# An Identity Revealed

# An Identity Revealed

BY Jared Larsen

RESOURCE *Publications* · Eugene, Oregon

AN IDENTITY REVEALED

Copyright © 2024 Jared Larsen. All rights reserved. Except for brief quotations in critical publications or reviews, no part of this book may be reproduced in any manner without prior written permission from the publisher. Write: Permissions, Wipf and Stock Publishers, 199 W. 8th Ave., Suite 3, Eugene, OR 97401.

Resource Publications
An Imprint of Wipf and Stock Publishers
199 W. 8th Ave., Suite 3
Eugene, OR 97401

www.wipfandstock.com

PAPERBACK ISBN: 979-8-3852-0236-2
HARDCOVER ISBN: 979-8-3852-0237-9
EBOOK ISBN: 979-8-3852-0238-6

VERSION NUMBER 02/05/24

Scripture quotations marked (NIV) are taken from the Holy Bible, New International Version®, NIV®. Copyright © 1973, 1978, 1984 by Biblica, Inc.™ Used by permission of Zondervan. All rights reserved worldwide.

This book is dedicated to all those across the world, who helped me along the way of my 4 year journey. I could not have made it without you guiding me, encouraging me and empowering me, each step of the way. Though your names are not mentioned, as there are a great many of you, know that I hold a special place in my heart for each one of you.

# Introduction

THIS BOOK WAS SPECIFICALLY designed for those who desire to go deeper into the Father's heart. For those who desire to solidify their Identity in Christ and to fully know themselves as they were always designed to be. To know oneself and become self aware is never an easy task, this book is designed for those who desire to take on this challenge.

What you are about to read, is a culmination of 4 years of travels throughout various nations of the world. Some of the events are personal as they took place on some great adventures, while at other times I am addressing topics/issues from my own perspective. There are times when I am vague as far as who I was with, where I was at, or my purpose in that nation. This is to protect the identities of those involved, but rest assured everything is completely accurate. You may find at times the things I talk about are hard to understand as they seem Pentecostal or spiritual. I want to encourage you to be open to the ways and means in which the Holy Spirit works on people and not be closed off or stop reading. I have found on my journeys that the Spirit truly works in mysterious ways that we often do not understand when looking at things through a logical lens.

INTRODUCTION

## Key Terms:

I.D: Identity (AKA: Value, Meaning, Worth, Approval)

Inner Healing: Process of working on various issues within ones heart, mind, soul and spirit that are holding you back from a deeper relationship in Christ. Usually lead by other people, some methods include Sozo or Elijah House.

## Why is Identity important?

It is my personal conviction that when humanity sinned and was cast out of the Garden of Eden, that we not only lost our relationship with our Creator, we also lost our Identity, our sense of who we are in God. We lost our place as royal heirs within the Kingdom of the Living God. Though I have no Scriptural support to base my assessment on, it only makes logical sense that we lose our sense of who we are when our relationship with our Creator is tainted. The problem I see in the global church is that we think that by accepting Christ as our Lord and savior, that our right relationship, knowing God deeply, and our I.D. is automatically restored. However I do not see this as being the case. I believe we need to cultivate our re-found relationship that we have with God. We must immerse ourselves in the Scriptures, communicate with God, and seek to know Him in the ways Adam and Eve did as well as those who walked with Christ. If we are not willing to do this, then in my own opinion we do a great disservice to the cross of Christ, as we only accept God but never fully know Him or our true selves. An example of this would be correlating it to marriage. If all you did when getting married would be to go through the ceremony and say "I do", then go your separate ways, would anyone want to get married? Probably not. But this is how the church, at times, treats our relationship with God; we enter in that relationship with Him by accepting Him (saying "I do") and then we go back home. We fail to venture into the honeymoon; we fail to dive deeper into an intimate heartfelt relationship with

God where He works on our hearts and mindsets and transforms our old Identity into His Identity. It is here, deep in the Fathers heart that we discover who we truly are as His sons and daughters, and step out with royal authority.

It is not enough to simply accept Christ, go to church, pray, tithe, worship, read Scripture, and think that by doing all of this we know God and have reclaimed our stolen I.D. from the enemy. Please hear my heart on what I just said, I am not saying that people who do the above list are not saved, but rather they endanger themselves of living under the orphan/slave/servant mindset or spirit.

It is for this reason that we must be intentional about seeking God, and knowing who we are in Him, and who He created us to be. It is only when we do this that we embark on a journey that few will ever dare to take. Why is this? I personally believe it is because so many people are afraid to hear from God or to make changes in their personal lives. But for those that go beyond mere salvation and move into the honeymoon and marriage phase with God, they will experience a love, depth, and intimacy with Him that puts all other loves to shame. To truly understand our I.D. in Christ we need to move past the surface level relationship with God and go deep into the father's heart. We must go so deep into His heart that we lose consciousness of who we are and enter into who we were always meant to become. We must first step out of the darkness and into the light and then move further into the light. By doing this, we allow the Glory of God to penetrate our hearts and break the things off of us that are not of Him, thus we are conformed to the image of Christ. We begin to shed off layers of our old self and all the things that we once found comfort in and who we thought we were. We are then clothed with Christ's I.D. and hold the title of sons and daughters of the Most High!

## Ask yourself:

You may be wondering, do I find my I.D. in Christ? Is my value, worth, approval and ultimately the essence of my existence found

## INTRODUCTION

solely in the living God? There are some questions I want you to ask yourself that may help determine if you are finding these things in God or in the things of the world:

- Am I finding that I always need to have the newest/best of everything to be satisfied?
- Am I never content with who I am in life?
- Am I finding my Identity in my nation, tribe, ethnic group, etc?
- Am I people pleaser? Do I say or do things to make others happy when I myself am not happy?

If you answered "Yes" to anyone of these questions, you probably have some identity issues that need to be worked on.

# Chapter 1
## The Adventure begins!

On June 14th 2009, I packed my bags and headed out into the great unknown in the Holy Land (Israel/Palestine). I had just finished my Masters degree in Christian Thought at Bethel Seminary and desired to travel. I wanted to see the land where God had done so much, and learn from Him and the people in that region of the world. So I left my job with Bethel Security during a bad economy, vacated my apartment, said my goodbyes, and left. Little did I know what God had in store for me! This whole venture that He was leading me on, was just the beginning phase of restoring my I.D. and bringing me into sonship/ the right relationship with Him.

During my three months in the Holy Land, God worked on my heart and used various people to chip off the rough edges that needed to be done away with. I met several people who were very prophetic and spoke Truth into my life and brought healing and insight where needed.

One person I met told me that there were parts of my heart I had not surrendered to Him yet and I needed to do so. I didn't exactly know what she was talking about, but it would be revealed to me over the next 4 years. It was shortly after this that God gave me a picture in my head while praying, it was of Jesus knocking on the door of my heart saying, "Let me in Jared, let me in, I want to heal you". Even though I had accepted Christ long ago I began to realize that there is always room for improvement/healing, if we are willing to let Jesus into those areas of our heart that are deep and personal. None of us are perfect and we need to first recognize this, and then we need to open all the doors of our life to God in order to be healed and be made new. I want to encourage you to be open to the Holy Spirit's ability to reveal the things within us that God desires to deal with, and allow the blood of Christ to cleanse and heal those issues brought into the light. Invite Him into your heart, ask Him to show you the things that must be dealt with, and allow Him to do surgery.

A couple weeks later I met someone from Hawaii who was gifted at inner healing. This was my first experience with inner healing and working on things of the past. We sat down and it seemed like a simple counseling session. All I did was close my eyes, and she walked me through the process of seeing where Jesus was at different times/points in my life when there were challenges or times when the enemy had attacked me, or times of hurt/pain in life. Some sessions were hard at times because it required me to be open, honest, and in tune to the Spirit's leading. As you move forward in being open and vulnerable with God, please recognize though it may be challenging, the amount of good that can come out of this process far outweighs the bad. You may have to dig up things from the past and deal with them so that they no longer hold any bearing on who you are becoming. This is a life long process of growth and spiritual maturity.

A few weeks later I met someone from south Africa who spoke about the Holy Spirit and His role in our lives. His message spoke deeply to me as he personalized the Spirit in a way that no pastor/professor ever had before. The role and significance of the spirit became more evident for me in that I needed to relate to Him as I did a normal person. It was this relational way of thinking and interacting with the Spirit that would be intricate to my personal growth. The more I opened up to the Holy Spirit and allowed it to work in areas of my life that needed healing, the more I found how gentle the Spirit is in bringing restoration to one's life.

While in Jerusalem, I met a couple that hosts a house of prayer. It was here that I was able to soak in His presence while they had praise and worship music playing. It was here God lavished His love on me in the form of the Spirit. It was important to take this time and just enjoy His presence while working on I.D issues. As you press forward with working on the things God desires you to work on, remember to take time to bask in the Kings' glory and rest in His presence. It was also here that I met a worship leader who was an amazing musician. He had a great deal of insight when it came to worship music, humbling ourselves, and reaching out to God. One of the main things he said hit a cord with me. He talked about how people react when he plays the song "Amazing Grace" and how they weep when he sings of how "amazing grace saved a wretch like me." He said most people are not crying because they recognize the amazing grace of God that has saved us, but rather because they are a wretch. It hit me like a ton of bricks, how often had I or others in the church cried out when hearing that song but for the wrong reason. We cry out because of our depravity not because of Christ and His amazing grace at work in our lives. We choose to remember our sins more and their effects on our lives rather than the work of the cross and its impact on our lives. If we desire to grow with God, we must move past this point of wretchedness and into the knowledge that His saving grace has taken care of all things of the past. Then we can weep with rejoicing for all He and his amazing grace have done for us.

Towards the end of my time in the Holy Land, I met a crazy Texan who was very encouraging. She said that when she saw me, the word "Royalty" was written on me. This is very significant in that to be a member of a royal family means that you must be an heir. You must belong to the royal families lineage/bloodline. To be a member of God's royal family, means I have direct access to the Father at all times whereas orphans, servants or slaves have no access to Him. What I mean by these 3 terms is that of a mindset, we live as these three and remain less than what we are both in thought and in action. But for being a part of God's royal family to have any meaning, I had to take it and own it for myself. With everything that God speaks to you, I want to encourage you to take ownership of it. Be it the hurts and pains of the past, the mistakes we have made, or who we really are in this world.

This beginning phase of my adventure was one of amazement and transformation. God was at work in ways I had never experienced before and I loved it. Little did I know the journey had just begun, and that the next 4 years would be a time of deconstruction and rebuilding, surgery, wandering through valleys, and climbing mountains. Yet the end result would be one of rebirth and wholeness.

# Chapter 2
# Who Am I???

## Adoption

I HAVE A UNIQUE background due to certain significant events in my life. I was born in India, raised in MN, grew up eating lutefisk (Norwegian fish), raised by a single mother as she never married, and grew up in a small white community of 700 people. So the question that stems from all of this becomes, who am I? This is a question that we all at one point in our lives should ask ourselves, if we truly desire to know ourselves and grow. A simple yet complex answer for me is, "A Son of the Most High God!" Yet there is so much more to this answer that I needed to grapple with and slowly unpack. I do not regret the life I have had as it has come with great challenges and great rewards. I may even dare to say that it is because I grew up without a physical father in the house that I was then forced to search for my true I.D. and eventually I found it in Christ. How many people do you know that have less of a crazy upbringing than mine and yet are still searching for their identity and are trying to figure out who they are? How many people go throughout their daily lives searching for meaning, significance and do not know true peace because they do not know who they are? It is only when we begin to trace our lineage back to God and see ourselves as His sons and daughters, that the missing pieces of the puzzle begin to fit into place and we recognize the person in the mirror. Jesus once asked the question in Mark 3:33-35, "Who are my mother and my brothers?" He then looked at those seated in the circle around Him and said, "Here are my mother and brothers." The point He was making in this text is that it is through Him that we are all adopted into His family and have a royal lineage. We are part of a royal family that is held together by the blood of God Himself. He chose to adopt us and this is significant in the fact that He did not need to but desired to. Unlike many other people in this world, I have the privilege of being adopted twice, once by my mother and a second time by Christ. The first one was through legal means while the second was paid for in blood. This adoption into God's family only holds weight for us if we fully realize its ramifications. We must be willing to live our lives as sons and daughters of the King. If being adopted into God's family merely means attending a church once a week then we have missed out on receiving and understanding our true I.D. We must live as ones set apart with an I.D. and an understanding of who we really are so that others may find their I.D. in Christ. We do this not with a prideful mindset or as people who have all the answers, but rather as mercy-hearted children of the King who bring healing and restoration to those with a lost and misguided I.D.

But what else does Scripture tell us about adoption? Let's take a look at Romans 8:14-16. "For all who are led by the Spirit of God, they are the children of God. The Spirit you received does not make you slaves, so that you live in fear again; rather, the Spirit you received brought about your adoption to sonship. And by him we cry, *Abba*, Father. The Spirit himself testifies with our spirit that we are God's children."

Your true Father is making it very clear that you are no longer under the Spirit of slavery or bondage, but now you are under a Spirit of adoption. We have the right to cry out to God at anytime. We have the privilege of being called beloved sons and daughters by the one true God whose Spirit speaks loud and clear that we belong to Him. No longer are any of us to be held captive by fear, a fear that grips the soul of mankind and plagues us with uncertainty of who we really are. The fear that once held you and I in bondage of never knowing who we truly are, of wondering if we truly "belong," or if we have been forgotten no longer holds any weight upon us as we step out with this spirit of adoption.

## How do you see God!?

As I continued to process my Identity, I had to ask myself how do I see or relate to God? This is something I continually ask myself as I learn and grow in this life, in order to see if how I relate to God is progressing or decaying. Many times, people will struggle with their I.D. and finding it in God because of how they see God. There may be "blockage" in a person's life because of their past experiences with Christians, the Church, their parents or authority figures. When we have negative experiences, we tend to have "blinders" or "lenses" on that will cause us to see and relate to God in a negative way. If we want to truly be free in Christ, we must work on the things of the past that are holding us back and causing us to see and relate to God in these negative obstructive ways. There may be various pictures we have of God because of our experiences and background. But if any of them portray God in a negative way, then those experiences need to be dealt with. You may have had adverse experiences at home with your family, or in a church that is legalistic, or maybe even with how different people mistreated you. All of these experiences can hinder us in our walk with God and in how we relate to Him. As a result, we may see God as distant, absent, authoritative, abusive, performance driven, spiteful, hateful, vengeful, always displeased, etc.

    An example of this from my own life, is that I grew up without a father in the house, as I mentioned earlier. I was adopted by a single mother, and so when it came to relating to God, He was in my mind "distant/absent". No matter how many sermons I heard about God being a loving close father or how many youth group lessons I sat through, in my mind God was still up there, and I was down here. I was living my life while He was off caring about more important people or busy with things. This mindset in my opinion is something a lot of people wrestle with. Often they have a father in the house who is physically and/or emotionally absent as well. The absent/distant father figure is very common in the American culture, with many kids growing up in single family homes, or living with parents who are always busy with work trying to make ends meet. It is no wonder that people today and in the coming generations will see God as distant, absent and even uninterested in their lives. Yet this is not the true heart of the Father.

In order for me to strengthen who I truly am in Christ, I had to work on this issue in my life of how I saw God. I had to look back at all the times I thought God had abandoned me or was absent. I had to ask Him where He was during those times. And what He revealed to me was amazing! He showed me how He had been with me since the day I was born and that He had always been walking with me through all of the mountain top experiences and through the deep valleys as well. Once I accepted this realization of God, my blinders came off and I was able to move forward in my relationship with God. All I did was open up my heart, mind, and spirit to the Father, then invite the Spirit of God to come with His presence, and then I asked God whatever questions I desired. I had to silence all the other distractions around me in order to hear His voice clearly. I had to be open to the different methods He desired to speak to me be it through words, impressions, visions, dreams, pictures, etc. It was only then I was able to receive from God the true image of the Father and His unending love for me. It was only in this place of openness where He could reveal to me how much He truly was with me all throughout my life. My preconceived notions of Him being absent or distant were mere lies from the enemy. Once I was able to see God in His purest form, I was then able to start to see myself through His eyes as a beloved son. It is only when we see the Father for who He really is that we are able to see ourselves for who we really are.

For some of you, you may see God as authoritative, a dictator, or a drill sergeant. You may have had parents who were very strict, rigid, harsh, and would get on your case over the smallest detail. As a result, you may think that God is up in Heaven just waiting for you to make a mistake so that He can strike you down with lightning. I want to encourage you not to see God as such. Rather, see Him in His true form as a gentle loving Father who instead of belittling you when things are not done right, lifts you up and encourages you to press on and do better next time.

I have found in my own personal journey that the true heart of the Father is compassion. God is the type of Father who is there with me at all times, leading, guiding and encouraging me in every possible way. When I fall down or make a mistake, He is quick to reach out His hand, help me get back up and encourage me to press on. The Father I now know is one who contradicts everything the world tells me about myself or about God. When the world tells me; "you can't do it," "you can't make it," "it's impossible," "your crazy," "you're a fool," "your not capable enough," "your not smart enough," "you're a failure," or any of the other negative comments it can throw at me, I know my Father is with me. His hand is on my shoulder, and He is gently whispering in my ear; "you can do it," "I am with you," "you've got this," "I believe in you," "keep going," "don't give up," "press forward," "I am with you my beloved son!" My friends, may you all hear these words from the Father and not the words of the world. I pray you choose to listen to the words that the Father desires you to hear, and drown out the words of the world.

**Helpful questions to ask:**

How do I see myself?

How does God see me?

What comes to mind when I hear the word, "Father"?

Where is my value and worth found in?

Am I influenced by what other people say about me, or what God says?

Do I see God as my enemy, laughing at me, discouraging me?

## AN IDENTITY REVEALED

Am I able to receive and accept God's love easily?

Do I enjoy talking with God?

Do I relate to God better in the form of an orphan, slave or son/daughter?

If you have any negative answers to any of these questions then you probably have blockage and blinders in your life that need to be dealt with in order to move forward with God.

## Chapter 3
## Home and back again!

AFTER MY 4 MONTH venture in the Holy land, I returned home and slowly recovered from my experiences as well as the food poisoning I received while in Egypt. Over the next few months I began researching into greater depth some of the things I had experienced while overseas. Most of these things had to do with the spiritual/supernatural and attempting to discern whether or not what I saw was legit or heretical. After seven months of research, I found myself being prayed over by a friend of mine from Seminary who was gifted in the spiritual/supernatural. As they prayed, I was spiritually baptized in the Holy Spirit and began speaking in tongues. This was a whole new concept to me and even explaining it can be a challenge at times. All I can say is that it was a God encounter/experience that radically transformed my life. Once this happened, I knew beyond a shadow of a doubt that I needed to return to the Middle East and continue on with the work God had started in me with learning my true identity in Him. I touched base with my friends in the Middle East and they said to come back and join them as soon as possible. I looked online and found a very cheap ticket to Amman Jordan. I booked it and three days later I was on a flight headed out on another adventure. Upon arriving in Jordan, I joined a very culturally diverse team that I learned a great deal from. It was here that I encountered more inner healing and learned from others' experiences and relationships with God. I learned how to be humble in being used by God, as there were times when I had to take a back seat and just "be" rather than "do". This was a challenge for me as having a Bachelors degree, a Masters degree and coming from the military, I wanted to be the one doing. And yet God was still working on where I should find my ID and in that teaching me to be content in just "being with Him". It was through these challenges I learned to sometimes be a supporter for what God is doing rather than always being in the spotlight. It was during this time that God was bringing to light and using my giftings to help others in ministry.

It was also during this time with this team I was given the opportunity to preach in a church about Identity and Idolatry. I talked about how we as human beings can easily find our value, worth, and approval in the things of this world be it our jobs, hobbies, finances, children, earthy possessions, etc. This opportunity allowed me to give back to others what I had learned about and worked through in regard to my own journey of sonship. The more we work on our issues in regards to identity and go deeper with God in the area of sonship, we may be given opportunities to pour into others and encourage them in their own walk.

One night while listening to a song called, "The Martyr's Prayer" I stared at a map of the globe and for some reason could not take my eyes off of it. I continually listened to this song all throughout the night and did not sleep as during this time the Holy Spirit was working on me and strengthening my identity in Christ. The spirit through this song was transforming my understanding of value, worth and what truly matters in the world.

It was after all of these experiences in Northern Jordan that I made a command decision to stay in the Middle East for the next two years and continue to serve on a ministry team while simultaneously working on my identity. This was a huge leap of faith for me, but I knew I needed to take it and I knew I would not regret it.

## Chapter 4
# The Hashemite Kingdom of Jordan!

### Spiritual guidance:

WITHIN THIS LIFE WE all need mentors and people who can come along side us in order to teach, train, lead and guide us. This also holds true in the spiritual life. We all need spiritual leadership that can come alongside us and raise us up in the faith and encourage us on our I.D. quest. You may call them spiritual mothers, fathers, brothers, sisters or mentors. The name ultimately does not matter. The point is to have those around you more secure in their I.D. in sonship/daughtership who can help you on your journey. Along my 4 year journey, God always brought various people from different walks of life to pour into me and help guide me in my journey. I would not be where I am at today had they not gone before me and cultivated their own spiritual life before ministering to me. I owe them all a great debt of gratitude.

In January of 2011, I started out on my two year venture/journey of self discovery; I served under 2 young American women who were extremely gifted in the prophetic, and I learned a great deal from them. When I say the word "prophetic," I mean that they were gifted at walking people through deep inner healing from trauma in their lives, being able to physically heal people, having God reveal things about a persons life to them, etc. They were like sisters to me, and though they were younger than me, they too were instrumental in my advancement towards sonship. I can recall many times when they would not just encourage me but also correct me, rebuke me, and keep me on the straight path. Because of their giftings in the Spirit, they could tell when something was wrong with me or needed an adjustment the moment I walked through the door. I developed a deep level of trust with them and submitted to their leadership. I can honestly say that I would not have the I.D. as a son that I have today had God not brought these two amazing women into my life. They had and still have permission to speak freely into my life at anytime. They have this permission to speak into my life because they first knew who they were as daughters of the king. Had they not had the depth and intimacy with the Father that they did, they would not have been as influential or been given access to speak openly in my life. They also have this permission because they were willing to take the time and build trust with me. I am telling you all this because there may be times in your own life when God uses people of the opposite sex, and/or who are younger than you to guide you on the path of sonship. I want to encourage you to be open to what they have to say and to listen to them not just with your mind but also your heart and spirit. You may hear pastors or other leaders say that this is not a healthy type of relationship because of opposite genders as well as the age differentiation, but I am here to challenge that notion. I have found that God is a creative God who will use anyone He desires to challenge you and take you deeper with Him. Throughout the Bible we find God using different genders and ages to speak into one another's life, therefore it stands to reason that He can still do so today in order to bring healing and restoration.

  During this time overseas, I met a man named Rei who had a great amount of wisdom and knowledge when it came to sonship. He became one of my closest friends who helped me along my journey. He was always willing to pray with me, answer any questions I had and even lead me through inner healing on past issues. He did this by sitting me down and asking guided questions that helped me to process and be free of any inner issues. If I was wrestling with any issues at anytime or even just wanted to hang out, I could call him day or night and he was there. He even gave me a few books that helped me understand sonship and what it truly meant to be an heir within God's family. He was able to speak into my life and be brutally honest with me when it came to issues concerning sonship. He was also someone I could test words of correction against as well as the Spirit's leading. What I mean by this is if other people would advise me to work on something in my life, or if I felt the Spirits prompting me to work on things, I would run it by him and see if he also saw the same issue in my life that needed to be corrected. He was someone who had authorization to speak into my life and correct me when needed as he gained my trust. We all need these kinds of people in our lives to make sure we are testing what is said, in order to make Spirit filled changes in our lives, rather than being a people pleaser and changing to make others happy. I recommend finding someone who has been down the road you are currently going on who can speak volumes into your life.

While serving in Jordan in 2011, I also met a visiting pastor from Texas who taught me a great deal about sonship and what it meant to truly be a son of God. We have kept in touch and periodically dialogue about growing with God and seeking God's best for our lives. He recommended several books and resources that helped me to understand the difference between being an orphan, slave, and son. What I mean by this is that we have the ability to see ourselves through different lenses and then project/live out these views. My friend helped me to see that I had lived as an orphan and a slave which caused me to always settle for less than I was worthy of. It also caused me to see my value, worth and approval as negative. Where as living as a son flipped all of that around and transformed my lens into a positive outlook in life. Though this individual lived back in the states, we were able to meet up several times in the various nations in the Middle East. Each time he had new teachings and resources for me on sonship and solidifying my I.D. in Christ. He was also gifted in the supernatural and in our times together, hosted the Spirit in such a way that brought healing and restoration to my soul. He was always encouraging in the area of sonship, and pressing forward with what God desired of me during the dry, difficult seasons.

No matter where I went in my travels, God had spiritual guides there waiting for me. Some were locals while others were foreigners, but either way, they all were an intrical part of my time in formulating my I.D. in Christ. They had great wisdom and insight when it came to restoration of the soul as well as dealing with the spiritual warfare around me. I not only had spiritual guidance throughout my travels, I also had it back here in the states as well. God continuously brought spiritual brothers, sisters, mothers and fathers into my life to point and direct me in the faith. God's faithfulness is truly amazing. No matter where we go, He is with us, and provides those who will spur us on in spiritual growth. Whether you are working on your I.D. or not, it is important to have spiritual guidance shape and mold your life. I want to encourage you to find those people who are further down the road when it comes to sonship/daughtership and let them minister to you. Listen to what they have to say even it if is hurtful or painful; learn from their experience and grow with the Spirit.

## For all the Prodigals

Some of you may have run from God and may be afraid to return to Him. You may think that you have fallen beyond the point of redemption, and that there is no point in returning to Him because He will never take you back. But is this truly God's nature/character? I don't believe it is so. As I began to think more in depth about Scripture and Identity the story of the Prodigal Son came to mind. I thought about the amount of times I had run from God and desired to live life my own way. If we look at the parable of the prodigal son in Luke 15:11-32, we will find a son who has hit rock bottom, and a loving father who runs to embrace his beloved son. But what is so significant about this parable that it would apply to us as sons and daughters? When we look at the parable in the original context/culture we begin to get a much bigger picture as to what is really going on. When the son goes to his father demanding his share of his inheritance, he is basically saying, "I want you dead, so give me my inheritance". The father grants his sons request and gives him what his son wants and watches him leave. As his son is out living life as he sees fit, he eventually hits rock bottom and ends up with nothing. We also find that no one was there for him, no one was giving him anything. It is like that many times with the world. We choose to find our I.D. approval, value and worth in the things of this world, but then when we are down on our luck and in need, the world turns its back on us, leaving us empty and hollow. But this is not the case with God as we clearly see from this message.

We find from the text that as the son returns, the father sees him and has compassion for him. The father then runs to his son which in the culture of the time would have been unheard of, for a father to run and accept his son who had desired him dead and now dares to return. Yet that is just what this father does; He runs to his son and just as his son is about to ask for forgiveness for his sins, the father puts a robe on him along with sandals and a ring. It is clear from this message that just as the father runs to his son, that God also runs to us. He runs with all His might when He sees us far off in the distance and does not stop running until He reaches us. He embraces us with the biggest hug we could ever imagine. He then clothes us with His righteousness, a righteous robe if you will. He puts a ring on our finger as a sign of our royal lineage/heritage. He throws the biggest party for you that the world has ever seen. He does all this in your honor, because He loves you and you are worth it.

If you have run from God, if you grew up hearing about Him but do not know Him personally, I implore you to run to Him with all your heart as He is the only one who can save you both in this world and the next. If you feel that your past mistakes or sins are too great and God could never find any value or worth in you, you are dead wrong. It is God who determines your value and worth not you, and you matter more to Him than you can imagine. It is never too late, whether you have been running for a few years or 50 years, it does not matter. He is ready to run to you with open arms. Let Him clothe you with His righteous identity, an identity that lasts for all eternity. Salvation is a free gift that costs you nothing, and with it comes a royal covering that the kings of earth would kill for. But you must take the first step in running towards Him.

There may be some of you thinking that because you grew up in the church, were baptized and confirmed in the church that you are good to go. Meaning that you are saved and bound for eternal bliss in heaven without needing to do anything else. You may be thinking that your salvation is covered because of all these things. I am sorry to tell you this, but that is not the case, as baptism, confirmation, etc are just rituals. Salvation can only come through a deep personal relationship with Jesus Christ. It is here within that defining moment that you step out of the darkness and into the light, knowing the Father in His purest form. Once you know Him in the purest form, you are then able to be clothed with His I.D. and loved as a son/daughter. Some of you may have even been hurt deeply by the church in various ways. To those of you I want you to know that the church is most assuredly not God. The church is made up of fallible people who continually make mistakes, and some of those mistakes end up hurting others within the body and cause us to walk away from God. It is my desire that you recognize the differences between God and humanity. Humanity's identity, the church's identity, is not God's identity. You should not feel compelled to return to a hurtful identity but rather go to God and receive a restored identity.

## All they have is the Military

For 8 years of my life I was able to serve in the military. One thing I noticed during those 8 years was that many people found their I.D. in the military. It became a common saying amongst many of us: "all they have is the military". This does not mean that we were mocking them as we too were wearing the same uniform and had taken the same oath as they had. But the difference was that they had formulated their entire being around the military. The very essence of their existence was pinpointed around being in the military and nothing else. The problem with this mentality is that they have chosen to only be known by the clothing (uniform) that they wear, and not by their creator. The interesting thing is how easy it is to get sucked into this mindset. After all, the military is great at instilling pride, honor, self-respect, self-discipline, and many other attributes into the heart and minds of people. When all of these attributes begin to be instilled by a secular entity, it is then easy for us to formulate our value, worth and meaning around that entity, thus causing us to live and die for them. It is very easy for Christians also serving in the military to fall into this trap and all of a sudden we are serving two masters. The problem with this is that when the two masters collide, who wins? The one who offers you the things of this world, or the one who offers you the things of eternity? If you ever choose to put on any uniform, I want to challenge you to not formulate the very nature of your being around that uniform or the one who issued it too you. Because if you do this, as soon as the secular entity no longer needs you, they will discard you, and your I.D. will be shattered and your world may be shaken. But I promise you this, if you formulate your existence around Christ, you will never be discarded, forgotten, or left behind. For God does not forget His children, He runs too them, fights for them, and even dies for them.

## Patriotism vs Nationalism

Along with analyzing my time in the military and realizing that I had tried to find my identity in it, I also began to differentiate between patriotism and nationalism and how idolatry can be found in them. There is a saying I heard once; "my country right or wrong". The problem I found here is that in patriotism we love our country yet we hold our leaders responsible and accountable for their actions, yet within nationalism we are prone to support the state no matter what the cost. The latter is a form of idolatry as we end up essentially selling our souls to a secular entity. The point I am trying to make here is that as believers we must be careful with where our allegiances lie. This sort of thing, in my personal opinion, was much easier for the early church as they were persecuted by the Roman government. But for us today it is a much more convoluted issue as we have freedom of religion and we are not persecuted. But where do we draw the line between the patriotism for the nation we live in and the loyalty for the God we worship/serve? The American church is at a fork in the road, in my opinion, one in which they will have to decide where they find their identity in; will they find it in God or in nationalism? My friends, I used to hold very strongly to the belief in "my country wrong or right," I used to believe that America could do no wrong therefore finding my identity in her was not wrong either. How mistaken I was. We cannot nor should we ever find our Identity in any nation. We can love the place that we live in and contribute to making it better but to become so intertwined in a nationalistic ideology can be very dangerous. Part of the reason I see it as dangerous is because we are giving power/credence to a secular entity and letting it do whatever it desires, possibly to other people who also find their identity in God just as we do.

Along these lines of "nationalism" and the all the issues it brings to the table when we choose to find our identity in it, also comes the issue of finding our identity in the current "staus quo" and not desiring anything to change. I have seen this greatly in recent times with people fearing that the United States is changing too much or too fast and thus voting/backing certain political parties that will maintain the status quo, thus ensuring that their current way of life will not be interrupted. I can understand the fears people have when the things they are accustomed to change before their very eyes. At the same time, to give in to that fear, makes absolutely no sense when as Christians our true citizenship is in heaven. What I am seeing in America especially in the American church is this fear that things are changing in various ways. Be it culturally, spiritually economically, or politically and this fear based viewpoint is causing animosity among all peoples in America. We have become a divided, fractured nation that was once a great melting pot. The church is playing politics in a dangerous way, one in which our image of Jesus is tainted and another where our identity as Americans supersedes that of our identity in Christ.

As I analyzed where/how I had tried to find my identity in, in regards to work, one key point in time stood out to me.

## The Mask

A great American tradition/holiday that many of us grew up with is a time to get dressed up and go door to door asking for candy. Every year millions of American children put on masks and go out trick or treating. Yet there are millions of adults who put on masks and never take them off. They do this for many reasons; comfort, stability, safety, the list is endless. These masks become the person's I.D. and consume one's life to the point that if the mask were to be removed it could shake their worldview. It will shake one's worldview if the essence of their existence has become so intertwined to the "mask" that they cannot conceive of "being" without that safety net. One mask that I wore was that of a security guard. While attending Bethel Seminary in St. Paul, MN, I worked for 2 ½ years for the security department. I enjoyed it so much that it eventually became part of my I.D. Now you may be thinking, how on earth can someone formulate their I.D. around being a security guard at a Bible School? The answer is a sense of purpose, direction, control, and authority. I was not just a student worker, I was a staff member who was in charge of the student workers for the night shift. I had total power over them and because the office was closed at night, no one had power over me. I was free to go where I wanted, when I wanted and tell all the other workers what to do. But it didn't stop here, because I lived on campus I would often work when I was not on the clock. I would ride around with other officers in the security vehicle or I would go to the "welcome center" at the main entrance of campus and do the officer's work for them without getting paid. I even once tried to work 72 hrs straight in one work week, most of which was back to back. However the chief of security caught me and finished that idea before I could even begin my 72 hrs of insanity. Without my I.D. as a security officer, I was lost, I did not know who I was or where I fit in. Please keep in mind the irony that all this happened while I was at Seminary studying about God and how to have a relationship with Him! Needless to say, when God told me to pack up and head to the Middle East, I was less than enthusiastic. Looking back, I now realize that had I continued on with Security, I would have lost my faith in God all together. The mask would have destroyed my relationship with my creator and my life. God had to remove me from my mask and place me in the "wilderness" in order to find Him and my true I.D. It is only 3 years later that I can honestly thank Him for removing this mask by having me leave my job. So what masks might you be wearing that you are not aware of? What masks need to come off so that you can look in the mirror and see the image of the Most High? Are you willing to let go of these masks and take a risk at discovering who you really are?

# — Chapter 5 —
# 2012 Spring-Fall

### Corporate identity

As I pressed forward in Jordan working with the ministry team and growing in my Identity, I ended up living with a group of Arabs for several months. All of them were from different nations, but I learned a great deal from them about corporate identity. In the U.S. we think of identity in terms of individualistic, whereas in different cultures, they think in terms of cultural identity. The Middle East is very much a warm culture in that they will immediately welcome you into their home and feed you, even if they just met you. If there is anything that you need, they will do all that is within their power to help you. This is life there, it is a part of who they are. Although cultural I.D. is very important, personally I would have to say that it is not as important than our I.D. in Christ. It is important to know where we come from, our cultural background, our heritage and roots, but these things should never supersede who we become in Christ when pushing ourselves deeper with Him. For example, my ethnicity is East Indian but my nationality is American. I have ties to two worlds, and though it is important for me to know both of those worlds as they are a part of me, they ultimately have no significant bearing on who

## AN IDENTITY REVEALED

I am. This is because who I am and who I will become can only be found in Christ. I remember my background, upbringing, and values but in the end it is the Christ who defines me, nothing and no one else. What does this mean for me? A great deal of things actually. It means that my ultimate allegiance is now to Christ, not to any nation, people group or political view. This means I am now called to a higher standard in which I am to emulate Christ to all people at all times. It means that when the nation I live in goes to war, that I am called to love my enemies and not take sides. It means that when I see conflict between two nations or people groups in this world, rather than take sides I am called to stand in the middle as a peacemaker and make disciples of both nations. Is this an easy road to walk? By no means! But when we are clothed with the I.D. of Christ we have a greater responsibility to the broken hurting world we live in where the lost need Christ. Though many of you may disagree with me on this, I want to challenge you to look at this issue from Christ's perspective. Did He really die so that our personal, political and cultural views could reign over everyone else's? Did He not die for all people groups, thus are we not all equal in His eyes?

My friends, I want to encourage you not to find your identity, value, worth or approval in your culture, as doing so will always let you down. Cultures shift and change, kingdoms come and go. Our allegiances must only be to Christ alone. If we become offended or take issue with Christians from other cultures/backgrounds coming in and immigrating with their languages and cultural norms then, I believe it is safe to say we are finding our identity in our nation/culture not God. The other reason this is significant is because it was during this time frame that the Arab Spring happened and out of no where there was chaos all around me. In a matter of weeks, people were rising up against their leaders and the leaders were fighting back. Their identity as a nation, as a people group shifted and morphed into something different. Out of these revolts we now have millions of displaced refugees who long for a home and no longer have the nationalism and to some extent the cultural identity, they once had.

Having an identity in Christ is the one thing we can hold onto when the sand shifts beneath our feet, or when our world suddenly erupts into chaos. The truth is, this can happen to anyone of us at any minute and in reality we should not be taken back or caught off guard when it does happen. Rather we should press on with our identity secure in Christ and help others to find their identity in Christ amidst the chaos.

## The Lost Identity of Israel

It was during my 3rd trip to Israel in 2012, I began to feel something I had not felt there before. It was a lost sense of one's I.D. Even though I had never felt this before, I recognized that as we learn and grow with God, He allows us opportunities to feel things in the supernatural that we have not before. What I was feeling was what the Israelis were feeling in their spirits. They knew who they were nationally, ethnically, and historically. But they do not know who they are as sons/daughters of the Most High. For this reason, their spiritual I.D. is lost until they recognize Christ, accept Him, and enter into a relationship with Him. Even though they may have the Old Testament, without accepting the full revelation of God embodied in Christ, they will remain spiritual orphans forever. We as Americans can actually go through the same thing. We can know ourselves as Americans, as well as a melting pot/salad bowl of cultures and ethnicities. But when it comes down to our true I.D. we can very easily remain lost. This can happen so easily in the American church and we don't even realize it. American Christianity can easily substitute an authentic genuine relationship with the Most High God for "Christian nationalism". We still end up going to church but now patriotism, prosperity gospel, and luke-warm messages fill our ears. We no longer are challenged to recover our roots, value, worth, or sense of being from the original image-bearer. We may worship God, but do we know Him not only as our Savior but also in a deep intimate relationship as Abba Father?

## Religion, Church, and Christ:

As I contemplated this issue of having lost ones Identity as I felt the Israelis were experiencing, the notion came to mind of finding ones identity at the opposite end of the spectrum, such as in religion or a specific church and the dangers posed with this. Now you may be thinking, what is the difference between them, as you may go to a solid church and be part of the christian religion, yet at the same time there is a difference.

The main difference between Christ and the church or religion is that having an I.D. in Christ is about relationship whereas placing ones I.D. in the other two will fail you. Placing ones value, worth, or approval in any religion will always cause you to fall short. You will never match up. Even placing ones I.D in the church will leave you empty and hollow as you are performing nothing more than rituals that have no eternal significance. It does not matter if you are placing your I.D. in Christianity, Islam, Judaism, Hinduism, Buddhism, or any other religion, they will all fail you. None of them can bring you to the place of sonship or daughtership in the Father. To find your value and worth in any religion will leave you unfulfilled and in a state of hopelessness. However, finding and even loosing yourself in the Christ child will bring you to a place of understanding fellowship and growth that this world cannot comprehend.

You may also be asking yourself, what about my allegiances to my tribe, nation, or culture? Do these also have equal weight with my I.D. in Christ? It is my own personal conviction that they do not. I would venture to say that our I.D. in Christ transcends any and all other allegiances. Our ultimate value, worth, and approval can never be found in one's tribe, nation, culture, religion, denomination, or ethnicity. It can and must only come from Christ alone. Though these group identities do have merit and value for people, they ultimately do not subersede ones loyalty to Christ. The reason for this is that it can become problematic to have dual allegiances to God and to anyone or anything else. Case in point would be a conflict between nations or people groups. If our loyalty to Christ is equal to that of our nation what happens when nations war and we end up with Christians killing Christians? This has happened many times throughout history and yet somehow we as Christians have always been able to justify it. We saw this during the American Revolution, the Civil War, and many other conflicts. Are we truly prepared to kill one another on the basis of "just war theory" or are we going to rise up as sons and daughters of the Most High and stand for something greater than our other allegiances? It is not possible to be sold out for Jesus and yet be willing to fight for a cause that politicians deem as legitimate yet simultaneously causes the death of our brothers and sisters. You are welcome to disagree with me, but it is my conviction that if our identity in Christ transcends all other loyalties and allegiances, then what more can we conclude but that we must let go of those previously held identities.

In January of 2012 my team decided to go to Dubai and meet up with the pastor from Texas that we had met in Jordan awhile back. It was here that he taught in greater detail about sonship and the difference in living as an orphan, servant, slave or son. His insight as to what it meant to walk into the light and live as a son pierced my soul and brought revelation to my own journey.

## Orphans

The orphan spirit/mindset affects each and every single one of us and we don't even realize it. We inherited this mindset from our original parents, Adam and Eve. When they choose to disobey God they took on the mindset of an orphan because they choose to no longer live with God, and so God had no choice but to cast them out. As a result we are now born with the orphan mindset.

All throughout the Scriptures, we can see the results of the orphan heart/spirit. We can see this in the relationship between Saul and David. In 1 Samuel 18:7-9, "As they danced, they sang: "Saul has slain his thousands, and David his tens of thousands." Saul was very angry; this refrain displeased him greatly. They have credited David with tens of thousands, he thought, but me with only thousands. What more can he get but the kingdom? And from that time on Saul kept a close eye on David. It was shortly after this that Saul turned against David and tried to kill him. We can see clearly the affects of the orphan heart that can even reside in kings. Saul had become jealous of David's success and became fearful of him. The orphan heart will always see things from the selfish point of view rather than from a son's point of view. Had he seen things from the sonship point of view, his response would have been much different. He would have recognized that both he and David were on the same team, they were both fighting for the same God. They were serving a greater purpose rather than their own ambitions and their own kingdoms. I believe this is one of the problems we face within the church today. We are so focused on our own ministries/positions within this world that we forget the bigger picture. We forget that we as Christians are all fighting in the same fight, for the same God. We allow the orphan heart to rule us and we become jealous of one another and at times resent God for taking other believers further than ourselves. If your response when you see others going further than you in life or ministry is resentment, anger or hostility towards them or God, then you may want to take this issue up with the Father and get things right. This does not mean that you are not trying your best or living up to your full potential but it may just be the "luck of the draw" that some are chosen before you and advance in ways you don't. This also does not mean that each time others advance before you that you have an orphan heart and have issues to work on. It is key to keep in mind that God uses us all in different ways and sometimes the ways we want to work or be used by God just doesn't happen for various reasons.

I have found that it is very easy for people who live with the orphan heart to keep a distance between them and God. They desire to know Him but only from a safe distance. This is a defense mechanism that is used to protect ones self from being completely vulnerable before an all powerful Holy God.

## Slave/ Servant vs. Son

As I moved out of the Orphan mindset, I began to also move out of the servant-slave mindset as well. There are a variety of ways in which we live in these mindsets and don't even realize it. It is just as unhealthy to live with the slave/servant mentality than it is the orphan one, as both hold you back from living as a son/daughter and living out your truest identity.

There was once a time when I wanted to get a tattoo on my wrist written in Hebrew that said "Master". The reason behind this was because I had a servant-slave relationship with God. I did not see myself as His son but rather His servant. Now there is nothing wrong with having a servant's heart but there is a huge problem in taking on the I.D. of a servant/ slave and not moving beyond this mentality into sonship. To be content in just being a servant/ slave means that we are willing to settle for less than what God wants to give us. God desires for all of us to step into sonship and be recognized as belonging to Him. To settle for anything else is to remain as orphans searching for our I.D. in a fallen corrupt world that will only fail us. When we choose to remain as orphans we will attempt to find our I.D. in whatever is most fulfilling/ satisfying. We may find it in relationships hoping that our significant other will fully complete us and we will be whole. We may find it in our children if we live vicariously through them. If we are an avid learner we may find it in academics. If we are in the ministry we may find it in serving in the church or on the mission field. It is easy at times for people who are serving God to mistake their service for their I.D. and soon they begin to honor/ worship their work for God rather than God Himself. For me personally, I tried to find my ID in the military, academics, various jobs, servanthood and even people. Yet when all of these things failed me, I was left with nothing because my I.D. was not secure in Christ. I was a believer, yet I was still searching for meaning and attempting to discover who I was? This is not to say that I did not benefit from my time in the military or my time at college and Seminary, but when these things became the root of my soul, I ceased knowing myself through the eyes of my creator and began striving for acceptance and approval from man-made entities. When God then sent me to Palestine for some specified training, my I.D. was shaken as I no longer had the military, a job, or academics. I had nothing to stand on or hold on too; even my health insurance was gone! All I had was a scorching summer heat and my Abba. My brothers and sisters please learn from my experiences, God does not need to send a giant whale to get your attention as He did with Jonah; He is very creative in His ways. If needed, He will use the most difficult, gut-wrenching, hellish experiences on earth to get you to turn around, seek His face and find your I.D. in Him. He is jealous for us with a passion that puts all passions to shame and He will not relent until our I.D. is secure in Him.

## Sonship/Daughtership

To live out our lives as sons and daughters of the Living God is to fully understand our position/ relationship with our creator and to know that we have complete access to Him at all times. When living out our role as a son/ daughter, we need to understand what this means. It is hard for our minds to wrap around the idea that the creator of the universe created us in His image, gave us free will, and then even when we blew it, He came to die for us. It can be hard to understand a perfect unconditional love that is never ending despite all our flaws and imperfections. So when I tell you that you are a son/ daughter of the Living God and can climb up on Papa's lap at anytime, this might raise some internal red flags or shake your theological view points when attempting to relate to God. Yet the truth is this is the relationship we have with God. We can enter His throne room at anytime and climb up on His lap and say anything that is on our hearts or minds. And because He is a good Father, He is willing to listen with ears wide open. We have His undivided attention.

I once heard a story of a soldier during the civil war who was attempting to get in to see President Lincoln but was not let in. As he sat and cried on the steps a small boy came up to him and asked him what was wrong. The soldier told him that he needed to be excused from military service in order to take care of his elderly parents. The boy told the soldier to follow him. He took him into the white house, past all the guards and into the President's office. President Lincoln looked and said: "What is it Todd?" The boy replied, "Dad this man has a serious problem and needs to talk to you". Only the son had direct access to the president. Only sons and daughters can walk directly into the throne room of God and make their requests at anytime. Only sons and daughters have the unique position that grants them access to the throne room without being stopped by angels, demons, or any other power. The question then becomes, "will we go to the throne room?" Are we willing to see ourselves as sons/ daughters and accept that position in our lives and enjoy this relationship we have with Father God?

During the summer of 2012 I returned to Minnesota from the Middle East and began to think about what it takes to change one's perspective about their identity. The transformation of one's identity cannot, nor should it be, only concerning the spiritual aspects of identity but also the mental and emotional aspects as well. Being that I am an academic at heart, I began to research the implications of refocusing our thoughts and restructuring our brains in relation to our identity and how one views themselves.

## Reprogramming our minds

The mind is a unique machine that has the capability to take in data continually and store it for future use. It has the ability to serve us well as we learn and grow in this world, but also the capacity to do a great amount of harm. If we are not careful, what the world is feeding us has the potential to taint our I.D. Just as the mind can store all of our fondest memories and time on this earth, it can also retain all of the negative moments and hurtful memories and cause us to see ourselves in an obscured image. You may also find when we look at Hollywood, the media, or advertisements, we find a standard that we do not match up to. Being perfect, fitting in, or being part of the "In crowd," teaches us that we are not good enough. We are trained to think that we need to be like everyone else, that we need to think like everyone else, and that we need to have everything that everyone else has. Our I.D. is subliminally tied into all of this and often we don't even realize it. Our mind tells us one thing because the world has told us what to think while the Spirit tells us something different. We battle mentally with listening to the world in attempt to matching up to an unattainable standard, while Christ is pointing to the Father and beseeching us to find our I.D. in Him. Decisions are already made up for us in advance and then programmed into our minds via the media. These decisions affect how we see ourselves in relation to each other, the world, and our creator. So how then do we reprogram our minds so as to find our I.D. in the One who made the mind? Science has proven that the brain can be structurally re-altered through mental practice. When we mentally think of those things good, pure and loving, the neurons in our brain which focus on these things grow stronger and affect our thought pattern. When we listen to the positive input from the Spirit about who we are, rather than what the world tells us, our mind is rewired to live out truth rather than falsehood.

Have you taken a test or done a project where you needed great focus? Did you notice that the more you focused on this one thing, all other things around you faded out? Even though all other things existed in your worldview, your attention shifted and you re-wired your brain to focus on what was most pertinent at the time. although we are bombarded by the media and content that affects our self-image, self-worth and I.D, we have the mental capacity to tune these things out and focus on Christ. God has given us the mental capability to overcome those obstacles that threaten to hinder our I.D. I want to encourage you to seek God for wisdom and understanding as to what humanity's true I.D. should look like, when attempting to rewire your brain. I also want to present to you some basic questions that may help guide you in reformulating your I.D. 1. How often do you go to God and ask Him to reveal to you your true I.D.? I promise you this, He never grows tired of it, but rather takes great delight in it. 2. Have you asked Him what things of this world have replaced/ tainted your true I.D. and then surrendered them to Him? 3. Have you made a continuous conscious effort to see yourself and those around you through the eyes of Christ and treat them as such? 4. When the enemy comes in and speaks lies against your I.D. in attempts to get you to return to the world, do you listen to him or rebuke him?

I want to open up to you a little bit in hopes it might shed some light as to what I am talking about. If you have ever met me, you would realize I am not exactly the tallest person in the world. According to the U.S military I am 62 inches tall. I can choose to formulate my I.D. around this fact and say that I am not tall like people in the media or around me. I can look at myself through the eyes of the world as small and unnoticeable therefore I have no value or worth. I can choose to listen to Satan who says that God does not love you because He made you short/ insignificant. Or! I can choose to reprogram my mindset by listening to God as to what He thinks about me since He created me. I can then remove all obstacles of the world that have tainted my mind and see myself through the eyes of Christ. And finally I can rebuke Satan with 1 Samuel 16:7, "But the Lord said to Samuel, do not consider his appearance nor the height, for I have rejected him. The Lord does not look at the things people look at. People look at the outward appearance, but the Lord looks at the heart!". If we look deeper at this passage, we will find more as to why God is saying this to Samuel. Humanity will always look at the outside and judge people according to appearance. Yet the God we serve does the complete opposite, He looks at the heart and whether or not it belongs to Him. I find it funny that even a prophet of God like Samuel is susceptible to this judgment. He looks for the oldest, strongest, most likely to rule as king and thinks this is what God had in mind. Yet God essentially says no, not this one. There is something interesting in how God chooses people to serve Him. David was the youngest of all his brothers, a sheep herder, and yet God saw something greater in him, took him and used him for His purposes. This should be an encouragement to us all. No matter what the world sees when they look at us, God sees so much more.

## AN IDENTITY REVEALED

Our value and worth in the eyes of this world are limited to almost nothing. Yet in our Father's eyes there is no limitation.

As I followed this process with retraining the tainted areas of my mind, my true I.D. was established and reformulated in Christ. I now see myself as my Heavenly Father sees me and ignore what the world may say about me.

— Chapter 6 —
# The Return Home

ON AUG 22ND 2012 at around midnight, I arrived in Amman Jordan. As I stood up to grab my carry-on luggage and leave the plane, I said in my head, "Ok Lord, one more mission and I'm done". I was tired of the Middle East, studying Arabic and needed a break for a little bit. As soon as I had finished speaking, it was clear as day right in front of me in red letters, an open vision if you will; "*India*"! It only lasted for a moment, but that one moment was enough to shake the ground I was standing on. For the first time in my life, I was at peace with returning to my native land. Previously, I had no desire to go back to India as I didn't know anyone there. Now, I was filled with peace, a peace that only God could give, so I knew He had His hand in it. I also had no desire to ever go back to India because I was once told that if I ever went back there, that the Indian government could take me, put me in their military, and there was nothing the U.S. government could do about it. For this reason, I knew that God was leading me and I could trust Him. This also was the second time in my life that God had given me an open vision, so I knew He was speaking of something important. I processed this encounter with many of my close friends whom I trusted and knew would give me wise counsel. They encouraged and blessed me in where God was leading me. They even put me in touch with some of their friends who lived in India and who were coming to Jordan to visit. I began to email them and found out that they too were from Minnesota! It was as if God was making things easier and easier for me to go and be with people who were from my own state! I met with them while they were speaking at a retreat/conference in Jordan on the topic of "Increasing your faith". I found it ironic that just as God was leading me to India, He was also challenging me to increase my faith, which was very much needed for this great adventure that lie before me. It was also during this conference that they led a prayer/activation time. As we closed our eyes and asked God what He was increasing our faith for, I saw the flag of India waving before me. This was just more confirmation that God was speaking to me about going to India. Later on, I met with the speaker and I told them how I felt God leading me to India. They invited me to come and stay with them on the eastern side of India just above Calcutta. This was the exact location of where my orphanage was. Now I knew God was leading me. How else could all of these puzzle pieces come together so perfectly; to be able to go to India, stay with people from my own state, and be located directly above the city of my old orphanage. You may not think this is such a big deal, but if you ever travel to India, you will quickly find that it is a huge nation. For me to be located above the one city that had significance for me was of vital importance.

  I finished up my time in Jordan, said my goodbyes, and on Jan 17th 2013, for the first time in 31 years, I headed back to India. It was as if God gave me favor each step of the way. I was not asked any questions by immigration when entering India. They simply stamped my passport and let me go. I was concerned because I look Indian yet have an American passport, and my passport says that I was born in India. I first spent a week in Mumbai (Bombay) and enjoyed seeing bits and pieces of the country. I then headed to the Eastern part of India to meet up with my friends from Minnesota. While in North East India, I stayed with some local Indians, which was a special treat for me as I desired to learn more about the Indian lifestyle/ culture. Every day was a chance to eat authentic Indian food and drink chai tea. We also met regularly in the morning for prayer and occasionally to fast. I was able to learn from them my native culture, language and customs. They also showed me how to navigate my way around India when desiring to travel to different places. I also enjoyed walking around the city on my own in order to get to know the area/ shops better. I learned a great deal from them about what it means to be Indian. Some of them were from a Hindu background while others grew up in the church, so I was able to learn much from all of them about religious viewpoints in my native land. We enjoyed watching Indian movies together as we hung out. I was and still am greatly indebted to them for all they taught me and did for me.

While in North East India, there was a prophetic ministry team that came and prayed for many of us. They gave me many words of encouragement and knowledge. One of the things they said was that my returning to India was similar to Moses returning to Egypt; he left Egypt and then returned with the presence of God! "You too have returned with His presence. There is no shame or guilt on you, if there was at anytime, it is gone." It was as if God wanted to use me in my native land for something bigger than myself, while at the same time teach me more of who I was in Him. This actually made sense with a mental image God showed me later on. It was a picture of three circles with a dot in the middle. The first circle was the spiritual/supernatural. The second was India and the third was America. Because I am surrounded by all 3 circles, I operate out of the first circle to speak life into the second and third circle. As I push my I.D deeper into God, He gives me strength and power from the supernatural realm to do His will in the two different worlds that are a part of me.

A few weeks later I met a women who was like a grandma to so many and who happened to also be from MN. She was also very gifted in the prophetic and was given words of knowledge about me from God that He desired to pass along to me. She asked if I was willing to forgive my earthly mother and father for abandoning me. Now please keep in mind, that she does not know my background or story. So as soon as she started speaking into my life about things from my past and being adopted, I was all ears. I had prayed over these things before with other prayer teams, but sometimes there can be residue that still must be dealt with. The Spiritual and emotional ramifications for going through such an experience can still have a grasp on a person after many years. So I prayed with her and forgave my earthly parents for abandoning me. I then prayed for them that if they were still alive that they too would come to know Christ as I had. That they would follow Christ and make His name known in India. As I continued to pray through things, I felt as if weights were being lifted off of my shoulders and feeling alive like never before. As you push forward in seeking your I.D. in Christ, you may need to go through "Inner Healing," which is the process of letting things go that are holding you back in Christ and releasing forgiveness to people for past hurts and pains.

Even after meeting all of these other people and working on things of my past, God still sent even more people to work in my heart. I met a couple from South Africa who were also gifted in the prophetic. They anointed my head with oil, prayed over me and told me what God my Father saw in me as a son! Out of the many things they spoke over me, they made a few things clear, "I was a prophet to the nations, and that I was anointed, appointed and ordained." Their words of wisdom and encouragement helped me understand even more who I was in the Father and all that He desired for me. I actually spent a great deal of time with this couple who became like a brother and sister to me. They were always willing to pray for me and speak words of life from the Father over me. They also saw some spiritual darkness that affected me at different times, and so they prayed for me and rebuked the spirit. Ironically, this was the same day I felt the need to fast and pray in one of the tea gardens in India. As I was pressing forward with God on my own, He was using those around me to pray for me and fight along side me in the Spirit. I want to encourage you, as you press forward on working on things that hinder your relationship with God, to find people like this who are brothers and sisters who will challenge, encourage, and lift you up along your journey. Do not try to go at it alone, for you may very easily regress rather than progress. The spiritual realm can be quite the war zone.

It was shortly after meeting with the these people and working on things, that while sleeping I had a heartfelt dream. God often speaks to me through dreams, but this one was different as it had to do with my I.D. It was 2 clips from the movie *The Lion King*. The first one was of Simba talking to his dad who was in the form of a cloud, when his dad said, "You are my son!" Immediately then the second clip came which was of Simba walking up Pride Rock and Simba's dad saying from heaven, "Remember who you are." I then woke up. I knew the message God was giving me. God was clearly speaking to me that I was His son, and that I needed to remember that. But if we dig just a little bit deeper, there is more. As I watched the scene in my head of Simba climbing pride rock, we see the rain falling down and washing away all of the death and destruction that had taken place as a result of Simba leaving his rightful place. When we take our rightful place as his sons and daughters, the death and destruction in our own lives is washed away by the blood of Christ and His healing power!

During my time in India, I had the opportunity to attend a Christian conference. It was here where I heard a speaker talk about Identity and Sonship. His message spoke directly to my heart about who I truly am in Christ and who the Father desires me to be. It was as if his message was for me and me alone as every word from His mouth brought healing in my I.D. and restoration in the area of sonship. He spoke of the Father's true heart for His children, His compassionate love for us, and His desire to be known by us. My heart was pierced by his message as he spoke of his own personal journey of sonship along with his invitation to come forward to receive prayer and healing from the Father. Anxiously I went forward. When I reached the front of the stage, I dropped to my knees and began to cry out to God, to know Him as Abba Father. It was during this time on my knees that a friend of mine came and put his hand on my back. He began to pray for me and speak words from the Father. They were words of healing and restoration. He stood in the gap for my earthly father and asked for forgiveness for never being there for all of my accomplishments, achievements, and my ups and downs in life. As he spoke, it was as if God was pouring out His Spirit upon me, and the things of old that I used to find my identity in were being washed away. They no longer held any bearing on my life and they were no longer significant. The only thing that mattered was being and living as God's precious son! It was during this time on my knees that God reminded me of things I had said or done that affected me in finding my I.D. in Him. Sometimes in life when we find our I.D. in other things/people, we end up making vows that affect us in unhealthy ways. Words are very powerful; they have the ability to act as blessings or curses. You may not believe this but it is true. Words can greatly affect where one finds their I.D. or approval. I had done this many times as I desired to know who I was and where my self worth came from. In doing so I had made "vows" or "oaths" that hindered me from living a free life in Christ. While on my knees crying out to God, I had to renounce these vows/oaths and surrender them to Jesus. If you have ever cursed yourself with negative words/comments or made unhealthy vows or oaths, I implore you to pray over them and remove them immediately. The way I did this was by repenting and asking for forgiveness for negative words or thoughts I had of myself long ago. I surrendered the fate of my life to the Father regardless of the cost or the outcome. While up in front of the stage, it was as if I had stepped out of the man-made light, into a greater heavenly light! It was the refiners fire of being made whole again, and it was a beautiful thing. When you reach that place of brokenness like I did, it is indescribable. Your flesh dies as the Spirit tastes everlasting life.

    At this conference there was also a prayer team that I met with and they prayed over me. One of the things they had me do was pray through some things of Hindu background. For me this was significant because I do not know my birth parents' background but I am pretty sure they have Hindu roots. Therefore it was important for me to pray over my past lineage/heritage with the blood of Christ and form a new lineage in God. One of the things that they prayed over was called the kundalini spirit. It is a Hindu spirit that affects a great amount of India. As they prayed, I felt God's Spirit working on me internally. I knew that even though I had not grown up in India, the simple fact that I was born there still held significant bearing on my life. For this reason it was imperative that I press forward renouncing any unknown vows/connections I had to Hinduism through my birth parents. As the Spirit worked on me, I could feel freedom in Christ. I knew what I was experiencing through these prayers were very real. It was then that I prayed and formed a new lineage in Christ, one that was pure and holy. No longer would I have any spiritual claim to a pagan lineage that did not acknowledge the One True God. From that day forward I would walk/move from a lineage that came directly from Christ and none other. If you do know your lineage and it is not a holy one, for example if your ancestors were into occult practices, witchcraft, freemasonry, Hinduism, etc... I would strongly encourage you to pray over your past, and reconcile it to Christ and form a new lineage in God. Cut off your old lineage with the blood of Christ and proclaim a new lineage free from your ancestors' past, one clothed in righteousness and purity. The team also gave me encouraging words from the Lord about who God sees me as and His activity in my life. One thing they mentioned that struck me was that whenever I take on a new assignment/mission from God, He is always asking for more volunteer Angels to go with me in what I do. This was very significant for me to hear because 99% of the missions that God has ever given me, I have gone on my own. It has always been just the Father and I traveling to various countries where we meet and work with various people. It was a comfort to know that for every assignment, God was asking for more volunteers within the heavenly realm to go with me as I worked on things with my I.D. As you press forward, know that even if you journey alone in knowing your true self, God is leading you and also sending volunteers within the heavenly realm to walk on this path with you.

It was also during this conference that I met an old friend of mine, Rei, from Jordan, who encouraged me to come to India as it was my birth nation. We met and discussed how things had been going over the last 3 months. I told him all that God had been working on with my heart and how He has been restoring my I.D. and teaching me who I am as His beloved son. We spent some time praying and God spoke through him to me on several things. One of the things that came to us when we were praying was a picture of a tree and a seed falling from the tree, rolling down a hill and growing into another tree. My friend and I came to the conclusion that the first tree represented my birth parents and the seed falling and growing into a tree was me. This picture was significant in that though my birth parents are a part of me, in the end I form my own roots and grow apart from them. I am not bound to them by their religious beliefs or spiritual bondage/ baggage. If any of you come from a background where your parents are not believers or there is spiritual bondage, know that you are not held captive to their bondage. You can be free in Christ and grow on your own. I also told him a few things I was experiencing and wrestling with. He reminded me that it was of vital importance to remain focused on my primary reason I came to India. His words of wisdom were refreshing and encouraged me to press forward in an attempt to find my orphanage.

It was also at this conference where I met another friend of mine who had once lived in India. He also encouraged me to take a leap of faith and go to India. He asked me how I was doing and if I was experiencing any "culture shock". It was not until he asked this question that I broke down and realized that boy was I ever! I had been so busy taking so much in from traveling around India that I had not realized I was emotionally and mentally overloaded from the culture around me. This was extremely eye opening as it felt like I was hitting a brick wall and didn't know why. I processed with my friend what I was feeling internally and the challenges of being back in a culture that I had not experienced for 31 years. Out of all the other nations I had traveled through, India was hitting me the hardest for some reason. It is difficult to explain, but I know it had to do with the fact that this was my native land. Although I was a foreigner in India, at the same time, I wasn't. All of the other nations I had been in I knew and stood out as a foreigner, but this time was much different. There were mental, emotional, and spiritual things hitting me that I had never felt before. My friend encouraged me to press forward with what God had called me to do/work on for the next 3-4 months; to press deeper into God and trust in Him. If any of you who have been adopted return to your native culture, be prepared to endure culture shock! Do not be discouraged. Continue to press forward in working on what God desires for you to deal with.

Shortly after the conference, I had the opportunity to travel with my MN friends to Calcutta. I was extremely excited about this trip, as this was one of the main reasons I felt God had lead me to go to India in the first place. After an all night train ride, we arrived in Calcutta. My friends went to take care of other things while I decided to venture out to find my old orphanage. I had the address of the orphanage, so I jumped into a taxi and headed out into the city. For those of you who are not familiar with Calcutta's population, it is about 4 million people. Being that I look like everyone there but do not know the language, is a bit of a challenge. However, I knew God was leading me and would give me favor. My MN friends also encouraged me by saying, "your Father goes before you." They were right I knew God had brought me to India for this purpose, so He was most certainly going before me. Prior to arriving at the orphanage, I prayed that God would have someone there to help me find it and get inside. Upon arriving at the street address, I found a man who happened to be a pastor at the church next door. He took me next door to what used to be my orphanage and a guard let us in. I explained who I was and that I was looking for my old orphanage from this address. The guard said that this building in front of me was it. Now, it was a nursing school. I looked and tried to think of what it may have been like 31 years ago with kids living in it and running around. Feelings and emotions hit me hard once again related to Identity. It was as if God desired to once again reveal much more to me about my past and who I am. Although I was not allowed inside the building because of the nursing school's strict rules, I was able to stay outside the building where I listened and talked to God. While talking with Him, He showed me what happened the day I was left there by my birth parents. He showed me how as they were leaving me at the orphanage, Jesus was taking me from their hands and embracing me tightly. God was clearly revealing to me that even though my earthly parents did not want me, He did! Even though they did not have the ability to care for me, He was going to. It was such an eye opening experience; God, the One True God had been with me every step of the way in my life, leading and guiding my path. I continued to process with God for many hours outside my orphanage, and allow Him to heal and speak truth into the areas of my life that needed it. To many people, this many sound strange or weird, but you need to remember that working on my I.D. was the primary reason I came to India. You also need to remember that my old orphanage was the only personal connection I actually have with India as far as my personal roots. I sent a text message to my friends back in Jordan who encouraged me to come to India. I told them where I was and of the restoration the Father was performing. They rejoiced with me in God's goodness and love. For some of you, going back to your place of origin or a place of heritage, may be difficult and challenging for you on various levels. I want to encourage you to do so anyway and to work on any issues God may bring to the surface. Do not shy away from Him opening up old wounds during this time. Rather, be open to Him doing "surgery" and bringing forth healing and restoration.

There is something else I want to pass on to you. Prior to going to Calcutta, my friends from South Africa told me that it was important not to stay "there". What they meant was that I could not remain in the orphanage spiritually, mentally, or emotionally. I had to leave the orphan spirit behind at the orphanage, and step out into sonship. If you ever return to your place of origin/heritage, leave the orphan spirit/mindset behind and step out into something greater. It is important to remember your past and where you came from but any spiritual, mental, emotional baggage must be left behind in order for you to enter sonship/daughtership.

Shortly after my time in Calcutta, I went up into the North East Mountains of India to meet with a team from MN called "Elijah House". They specialized in Inner Healing methods different from what I had experienced in the past. For two weeks,

God moved in my heart and spirit through this team to bring forth even more breakthrough in my life. If there is one thing I cannot stress enough, it is Inner Healing. If you ever have the chance to go through it, do it! If you want to be whole and complete in Christ, then you most assuredly will need to do some form of inner healing. We all have baggage from the past that needs to be dealt with. Some of us have more than others, but even the smallest amount, can prevent you from knowing your true self and living out your full potential in Christ. Going through Elijah House was the final phase God desired me to do in order to get rid of any and all residue of past issues that were holding me back in life.

My time in India was coming to a close as my 6 month visa was about to expire. I spent the last couple of weeks walking around the city and enjoying my time with people I had met and processing all that I had been through. I went way up into the mountains for a few days and just enjoyed the presence of God while walking around lush green wooded areas. It was refreshing to just have some time with my Father in green beautiful places and process all that I had learned. It was at this time I also had the opportunity to co-teach about relationships to a group of about 40 college students. I taught it with one of my friends from MN who had initially invited me to India. I taught how they could relate to God and how their relationship with Him should affect how they relate to other people. My friend then took it a step further and taught about relationships within a dating and marriage context. It was amazing to be able to be used by God in discussing relationships and relating to Him after all the work He had done on me and working on our relationship as Father and son.

If you ever get the chance to go to India, you will find tons of different gods/goddesses worshiped all over. You will see different statues/idols of the gods placed throughout the country. Anytime I walked by them, I felt sick to my stomach. God allowed me to feel certain things, in this case the dark influence of the demonics behind the idols. This affected me in a few ways. First, it stirred in me a desire to strengthen myself within Christ so as not to be affected by the demons around me. And the only way to strengthen

## AN IDENTITY REVEALED

myself in Him was to be known as a son. Once again, to know God deep and intimately in a relationship was the only way I was going to be able to deal with the warfare around me. Secondly, it caused me to be wary and cautious of the idols around me. I had to know my limitations when dealing with warfare, unless I wanted to get beat up spiritually. I had to be on guard so as not to surrender my progress to the enemy, and revert back to the orphan or slave mentality.

On June 15th 2013, I boarded a plane to head back home to the states. As I sat down in my seat, I was bombarded with so much emotion. I had spent the last 6 months in India experiencing so much and seeing so many parts of my native land. The amount of healing work and revelation that the Father had brought into my life in just 6 months was unbelievable. The culmination of working on my identity after 4 long years of travels was complete. It had been exactly 4 years to the day, since I left the states and began this amazing journey of identity, self-discovery, and Sonship which began in the Holy land and now I had finished it in India. I felt alive in a way I had never felt before! It was almost impossible to describe all that I had been through and what God had done for me, in me, and to me. Even now it is so hard to put into words such an adventure of I.D. and discovery that God brought me on. It was as if I had been born again. I had a passion, desire, and drive for life that I had never had before. The weights that I had felt before in life were completely gone. The issues/concerns that once dominated my life had been blown into oblivion. I was free! All I could do was laugh, smile, rejoice, and live life to the fullest. I now knew who My Father was, and I had become His beloved son. For the first time in my life, I wanted to stop living my life *for* God and start living my life *with* God. And yes, there is a huge difference between the two. Living my life *for* God was something I did as a servant/slave whereas living my life with God was something I would do as a Son. I now recognized that life truly is a gift, and each day is an invitation to go deeper into the Father's heart. Never again would I live with the mindset of an orphan, a slave or a servant. From now on I would forever live as His beloved Son. I would choose to dwell in the House of the Lord all the days of my life. All I could do, was thank God for all that had been done and encourage others to take a leap of faith and find their identity in Christ.

# Chapter 7

# Processing the mountain-top experience

WHEN YOU GO THROUGH on experience like I did, you need to take time to process everything you went through and I have found that it is best to do that once your outside of that element. For me, it was best to process my time in India after I had left and could reflect on all I had been through, and all that the Father had done for me.

### For those adopted

If you ever get the chance to go back to your place of origin, I encourage you to do so. Go back and go through whatever healing process the Lord desires to take you through. However, do not go back until you know beyond a shadow of a doubt that it is God leading you. I could never have gone back to India had He not been leading me. He had to build me up and prepare me for such a venture. If I would have gone before I was ready, the results could have been disastrous. For this reason, ensure it is the Lord leading you to go back and work on the things He desires you to deal with. I also want to give you a heads up as to what you may encounter, as

I experienced it in India. I will begin with this, "Full acceptance of ones-self does not equal acceptance by the world/other cultures." Just because you work on your I.D. issues does not necessarily mean that your original culture will fully accept you back into it. You may only be able to have a partial belonging. This of course depends upon how long you stay in your country of origin and the type of culture you are relating back to. When returning to your place of origin, you may find that you feel like a triangle attempting to fit into a circle (culture you grew up in) as well as trying to fit into a square (your native culture). It does not work well. You may find that you can only fit into the square up to a certain extent. For example, I fit back into the Indian culture in regards to the food as I love hot and spicy food, but not so much with the language, customs, rituals, and way of life. Eventually, I had to accept that I may never fully be accepted by my native culture, and that is ok. It is more important that I am accepted by Christ and His kingdom rather than any culture I attempt to mesh with.

## Rejection in the Womb

While traveling throughout the world, I learned about something that was very strange to me, yet the more I learned of it the more it made sense. There is something called "Rejection in the womb". It happens when a mother is pregnant and does not want to keep the baby. Because the baby is connected to the mother the child feels and knows this rejection subconsciously. Whether the mother keeps the child or not, the spirit of rejection has already affected the child without either of them realizing it. However, I also learned from those gifted in the prophetic that there is also rejection from the father that can affect a child. This type of rejection does not come from the womb but rather by words. A father's words are very powerful over his children. This rejection can dramatically affect children later on in life. When the child feels inwardly that they are rejected, or were never wanted, they may search out love or acceptance at an early age in the wrong places. There is also the potential for the orphan spirit, a spirit of rejection, or demonic influence to come into one's life at this point in time because of either the mother, father or both.

One effect I have seen from this type of rejection is that people will always feel unloved, undesired, and will even keep people at a distance so as to protect themselves. They will let people into their lives but only on a surface level; after that they will put up barriers in order to protect themselves from feeling the same type of rejection that they experienced from their parents. They may even believe that the people they have in their lives, be it friends or family, will reject them for various reasons. This can cause unhealthy emotions, feelings or even trust issues to develop. The result is a vicious cycle of fear, mistrust, and rejection of those around you.

The other effect rejection from the father and mother can cause is early unhealthy relationships with the opposite sex. If a boy is rejected by his mother, he may feel the need to receive approval, acceptance, and formulate his I.D. around women at a very young age. This may come in the form of sexual thoughts, desiring to be in a relationship, and even becoming sexually active at a young age. The same is true of girls who were rejected when they were young. They may have the tendency to receive attention from men at a young age in order to feel accepted. What you may also find is that those who wrestle with rejection from their parents, are never fully satisfied with any relationship that they have. They are constantly trying to gain approval from the opposite sex but ultimately are never fully satisfied. Thus the rejection they feel continues to grow and strengthen it's roots into the heart and soul. This becomes a vicious cycle that will continually lead to more rejection, hurt, pain, and anger until the spirit of rejection is cut off by Christ or until the person dies.

As a person continues to grow in their life, the spirit of rejection can also be continuously fed through other means. An example of this would be a person who was rejected in the womb, and then throughout their adolescent years are rejected by their peers. The orphan spirit, the spirit of rejection, feeds off of this and continues to do emotional, mental, and spiritual damage to the individual. The individual may always feel unloved, unwanted, undesired, or even see themselves forever as an orphan. If you are experiencing any of these things I want to encourage you, to seek help and receive inner healing from those equipped to deal with these issues. Though you may already be saved through Christ, rejection in the womb can still be holding you back to living your life completely free in Him.

## Jesus sees your value and worth!

If you still doubt your self worth and value, then maybe its' time to look more into the life and ministry of Christ. If there is anyone who knows your true value and the amount of worth that you have it is God. Lets take a look at Mathew 19:13-14, "Then people brought little children to Jesus for him to place his hands on them and pray for them. But the disciples rebuked them. Jesus said, let the little children come to me, and do not hinder them, for the kingdom of heaven belongs to such as these." At a time when other people are trying to meet with Jesus and children are being pushed away from Him, Jesus takes a stand for them. He makes it clear that the kingdom of God also belongs to them, it is not just for adults. He invites them to come and to be a part of His life, ministry and kingdom. He knows and sees their value and worth even when His own disciples don't. This should be a huge encouragement to us, because if Jesus is willing to take a stand for children and proclaim that they too belong in His kingdom, then is He not also willing to take a stand for us. Jesus sees you, and notices you even when the rest of the world to trying to push you out of the way. Even when the church is trying to silence you, Jesus is crying out, "let them come to me!"

If we also look at John 8:3-11, we find the Jesus also sees those who have been judged and mistreated;

> "The teachers of the law and the Pharisees brought in a woman caught in adultery. They made her stand before the group and said to Jesus, Teacher, this woman was caught in the act of adultery. In the Law Moses commanded us to stone such women. Now what do you say?

They were using this question as a trap, in order to have a basis for accusing him. But Jesus bent down and started to write on the ground with his finger. When they kept on questioning him, he straightened up and said to them, Let any one of you who is without sin be the first to throw a stone at her. Again he stooped down and wrote on the ground. At this, those who heard began to go away one at a time, the older ones first, until only Jesus was left, with the woman still standing there. Jesus straightened up and asked her, Woman, where are they? Has no one condemned you?

Here we find a woman who is being used by the religious authorities as a mere pawn in order to trap Jesus. But Jesus sees this woman and knows what she has been through and what she is experiencing at this moment. In this woman's mind, she probably knew there was no way out. There was no hope. Yet Jesus not only takes a stand for this woman in a unique way, but also challenges the religious authorities in their own self-righteousness. He simply asks the first one who has no sin to throw the first stone. To the religious authorities, they could have cared less about this woman; but to Jesus she was one of His precious children. He not only took a stand for her with His question to the Pharisees, He also forgave her sins. Jesus sees those who are being used, mistreated, abused by others, and notices that they have value and worth that the world does not notice. He restores their value and dignity through His forgiving love.

We also find in Luke 5:12-13, a man with a skin disease who desired to be made clean. In the time of Christ this man would been labeled "unclean" by his culture, society, and Old Testament law. But even so, Jesus the true lawgiver, saw this man's true value and worth and made him clean. We find here that Jesus reached out His hand and touched the man. You would not normally see this in that culture as you too would be considered unclean. Yet Jesus saw more in this man than his outward appearance. He saw a man in need and was willing to meet that need even if it broke the religious and cultural norms of the time. The true value that Christ sees in all of us is immeasurable. This is evident in His actions toward so many who society deems as "unclean or untouchable" For those of you who may be blind, deaf, mute, have a handicap or skin condition, know that Jesus sees you. He sees you whole, He sees you as He created you to be.

Having traveled throughout this world and worked with various different cultures, I have found that many people struggle with knowing their true value and worth at some point in their lives. Many of you are hurting, struggling, wrestling with various issues. You may often wonder if you truly have any inherent value or worth. You question if God has abandoned you or if heaven has turned a deaf ear. I promise you this; He has not forgotten nor will He ever forget you. Rather, He has been walking, running, and even fighting alongside you. He loves you so much that words cannot describe the amount of value and worth He sees in you. It is His desire for you to find your true self in Him alone and to know your intended purpose in this world. We can only do this through Christ and going to the cross, and asking for our true selves to be revealed. Just as He stood up for those 2000 years ago, He still stands for you today. He fights for your honor, value, worth, approval, your very essence with all that He is. And in the end may you hear Him say these words, "welcome my beloved, you are worthy, you are approved, you are loved!"

## Benefits of living as a son or daughter:

My brothers and sisters, if there is one thing I have learned on this journey, it is that there are huge benefits of challenging yourself and pushing your I.D. deep into the heart of the Father. When you know who you truly are in Christ, and the Spirit of God has transformed your inner being into a son/daughter, there is nothing that the enemy can come at you with that will destroy you!

You will recognize as I did that life truly is a gift from God and you will desire to live it to the fullest every day. Each day becomes even more precious as none of us know when our time is up here. You will desire to make each moment count for something more than yourself.

# AN IDENTITY REVEALED

One thing I already mentioned but want to touch on a little bit deeper, is the difference between living our lives *for* God vs. living our lives *with* God. One of the huge benefits I found when working on I.D. issues is that when we step out and live as the beloved son/daughter that He has called us to be, we start to see our lives and how we relate/ serve Him in a whole new light. When we live our lives *for* God, we can still be stuck in the servant mindset. Doing this can make ministry or even living life for Jesus draining, exhausting, or a seem like a task that must be done so as not to incur the wrath of a vengeful God. But when we start to live our lives *with* God, our mindset, paradigms, ministry, and our very life changes in a dramatic way. Life all of a sudden becomes this huge adventure, where we are limitless because of the God we know and the power He has. We now can see that it is never the destination that matters, but rather the journey of life and what we learn along the way.

One of the benefits I have found is that God trusts me much more specifically in the area of my "calling". He trusts me when it comes to ministering to others, serving them, and speaking truth into their lives. As we learn and grow with the Father, He will trust you a little bit more each step of the way to speak truth and healing into other peoples lives. This shows how we need to be even more dependent upon Him so as to use His gifts properly.

Another benefit I have found is that you will have a "peace that surpasses all understanding." There will be a peace and joy in your heart that is uncontrollable and it will flow out of you regardless of your circumstances. No matter how difficult times may become and how out of control life seems, the peace of Christ will rule your heart, mind and soul when you take your rightful place as the beloved son/daughter. It does not matter if there is total chaos all around me, because I know who I am in the Father and He is with me, which gives me great peace through turbulent times. Along with this peace comes a confidence, boldness, and fearlessness that is unbelievable. When you truly know yourself in the eyes of the Father, and have taken your proper place within

His royal court, there is something transformational that takes place within your being.

A third benefit I have found is that when you know who you truly are, you can't help but challenge others in their I.D. You desire for all others to find their value, worth, and approval in Christ alone. You want to bring out the best in people because you see the best in them. You recognize the untapped potential that they have and the capabilities they possess but they themselves do not know it yet. When you are secure in who you are within the Kingdom of God, you will begin to believe in those around you and desire to see them flourish within the kingdom as well.

A fourth benefit of living as a son or daughter as well as a challenge, I have found is contentment. I have never known such contentment as I do now. I am content with who I am and where I am at in life. Prior to knowing who I was in Christ I was never content with life, even though I was saved, I still was not content with who I was nor where I was in this life. But now, knowing who I am in the Father, I am content with all I have, all that I am, and who I am in Him. Yet at the same time looking back at where I was in life and who I was, I know there is still room to grow and improve. If God can take me to where I am at in such a little amount of time, what will the next 50-60 years bring if I pursue Him even more? So if you ask me am I content with who I am and where I am at in life, I can honestly tell you, yes and no. Because I know who I was and what I was like back then, and I know who I am now. I know who I am now and I know what I want to look like in the future. When you finally reach that point of self-awareness and know who you truly are in the Father, do not settle with just one step of contentment. Press even deeper with Him and reach a more intimate level of contentment with Him.

I now know and understand God's love so much more than I could ever have imagined. I also understand His mercy and grace much more as well. In all my years of being saved and knowing Christ, I never could have imagined experiencing such a deep love from the Father as I do when taking my rightful place as His son. I had always been told of how good God was, but I did not fully realize it until the end of my journey in India. The joy that I feel now is nothing I could ever have imagined or dreamed of. Nor is it anything I could have attained on my own, as it came solely from the Father's heart. My friends, God is so good, that He does not stop reaching out to us in so many ways so what we would have not only salvation, but be crowned as royalty. The depths of His mercies none of us can fathom, and for the creator of the universe to reach down into humanity and provide a way so that our right relationship might be restored in the midst of our sins, speaks volumes of the loving Father that we have. When you come to know Him as I have, may you be engulfed by His everlasting love. May the compassionate heart of the Father fill every fiber of your being.

## Fighting for our I.D.

During my venture I had to learn to fight for my true identity. I had to learn to endure and fight for what I wanted and who I wanted to become in order to truly be whole. I want to encourage you to develop a mentality of fighting for your true self worth, value, and image. Fight for your true identity and destiny.

    I believe that it is possible to lose our I.D. in Christ when we do not maintain the right relationship with Him. I believe that Christ beckons us deeper and deeper into the Father's heart daily. He gives us an open invitation to step more into His glory and be filled and receive our true I.D. in Him. To go deeper every single day with our Creator is a call to intimacy that most in the world never dare to dream about. It is an intimacy that puts all others to shame and certainly one that sons and daughters should delight in, rather than see as a chore. One of my favorite places to receive more of my I.D. is on a frozen lake in the winter time late at night. I love to go out on my own and seek my Father so as to pour my heart out to Him and receive from Him. I love answering the call of Christ to dive deeper into the Father's heart and find out, who am I? I do not close my eyes when I go out and talk to him on the lake, nor do I pray as if He is distant. But rather I cry out to Him loudly and listen to what He has to say. I walk back and forth all over a solid chunk of water while gaining more I.D. from the Creator. I do not regret one moment of freezing on the lake while talking to God as this is our personal line of communication. It has been this type of intimacy that has sustained me in my darkest hours, because it secured who I am in Him. This is where I am able to fight for my I.D. without end. So my challenge to you is this: find a time and a place that works best for your soul to commune with your Creator and dive in! See what new revelations God gives you about who you are as His precious son/ daughter from this intimacy. Fight for your rightful I.D. through deep intimacy with the One who knows you best.

## Protecting your I.D.

There may come a time in your life when you are required to protect your I.D. from others. What I mean by this is severing friendships/ties with people who are dragging you down, beating you up, or tearing you apart inwardly. It could just mean putting some distance between the both of you, not speaking to them as often. These people may be co-workers, close friends, people within your church, or even family members. Once I had my Identity strengthened in Christ, I immediately recognized the significance and importance of protecting it, so as not to regress. Since not everyone in this world is attempting to solidify who they are in Christ, you may have friends who are always negative and will try to turn every situation into a negative experience for you. As you are growing in Christ and discovering who you truly are in Him, they on the other hand are living under the "orphan spirit" and affecting those around them with negative viewpoints about their I.D. You will know this is occurring when you have peace with who you truly are in Christ and start speaking about it with others, and they in turn will speak out against you with the orphan mentality. These people may also bring up things from the past, or continually belittle you, "You should have tried harder, your efforts were not good enough, what were you thinking?" "You're stupid," or any other negative comment concerning your past to bring you down.

Now, it is important for us to learn from the past, but we cannot live in the past, especially as we are growing in Christ and dying to our old sinful nature/ways. Those who still live with the orphan mindset may deconstruct who you have become (son/daughter) and drag you down to their level. It's not that they are trying to do this on purpose, it's just that they have not found who they are in Christ and therefore want you to feel as they do and share there outlook on life. I have had this happen with other people who have also been adopted from various nations or were abandoned by their parents when they were young. They continually see themselves as an orphan who was abandoned by their biological parents and desire to live with the mentality of, "I do not belong". They live with the "orphan spirit" reigning over their lives and cannot bring themselves to rise above their perceived status and become the son/daughter they were always meant to be.

## Identity and Spiritual warfare

You may or may not believe in demons and spiritual warfare, but for me they are very real and relevant in regards to identity. What I have found when dealing with spiritual warfare/ the supernatural, is that the power and authority given by God, can only come from a deep intimate relationship with Him and knowing oneself within Christ. If I do not know who I am in Christ and if I do not step out and live as the beloved son that He has called me to be, then how can I expect the power of the Most High to work through me? The answer is, I cant! If I want to move forward in this world and do amazing things for God/with God, then I must be known by Him. I must push myself deeper into His heart, work on the things He reveals to me that are a hindrance in our relationship, and accept the calling and anointing He has on my life. When we do not know who we are in Christ as sons and daughters when dealing with the supernatural, we run the risk of becoming victims of a demonic attack when dealing with spiritual warfare. Now for some of you, you may not believe in demons or spiritual warfare, but for those of you who do and deal with it, I want to encourage you to push your I.D. deeper into Christ so as to not become a casualty of the enemy. Many Christians think that as soon as you accept Christ, the devil cannot touch you, and you are immune to spiritual battles. But I am here to testify that this is not the case. Accepting Christ as your Lord and Savior saves you from your sin, but does not mean that the enemy is going to leave you alone. On the contrary, you will probably deal with warfare much more once you have accepted Christ than beforehand. It is for this reason that I believe that you must secure your I.D. in the Father if you desire the Holy Spirit to work through you and protect you.

As I have continued to work on my I.D. and the things that were coming between God and I, the warfare only intensified. I say this to you as an encouragement. If you are under attack from the enemy while challenging yourself with God and desiring to know Him deeper, then you are on the right path. The more you draw closer to God the greater the battles you will face. The last thing the enemy wants is for you to reclaim the deep intimate relationship humanity had with God, that he stole from us. For this reason, you need to be aware of the fact that the enemy has many battlefields for us to cross through. Do not be discouraged but rather take heart, for Christ has overcome the world and will lead you through every battlefield that lies ahead. There may be many nights where you don't sleep because of spiritual attacks. You may wake up at night feeling the presence of demons all around you, and they are trying to tear you apart from God. You may encounter various kinds of sickness that afflict your flesh and weaken you greatly, and yet your spirit is still in tact. Thoughts from the enemy may even fill your head with doubt, mistrust, and questioning God. Thoughts of failure or a sinful past may creep in and make you wonder if you can really withstand this battle.

It was during my first venture to Hashemite Kingdom of Jordan that all of these things, and much more happened to me. I encountered a team there who knew spiritual warfare at a greater level than I did. They felt God leading them to instruct me that my identity and approval must come from Him alone. Then they prayed for me and things were broken off of me within the spiritual realm that I cannot explain. How do I know this to be true? Because instantly I was on my knees dry-heaving, and I could feel something come up from the pit of my stomach to my throat and out of my mouth. Does this mean I was demon-possessed? No, but it does mean that there were spiritual attachments that were hindering me and holding me back in my I.D. in Christ. I am telling you this not to freak you out about demons and having them attach themselves to you, but to make you aware there may be times when you need to have one of them removed that has attached themselves to you. Please do not be afraid of this process, as it is much needed to feel a greater freedom in Christ and to know one's true self.

When encountering this war zone and fighting for your I.D. there are a few things I have learned that may also benefit you:

- Talk to God out loud as if He were right next to you. Be open and honest with Him with what you are facing/going through. Cry out to Him in your time of anguish.

- Keep a journal of all that God has done for you in the past, and all the words He has spoken to you, and look back at it often as a reminder of His faithfulness in your life.

- Never fight alone, always have other people praying for you and keep in touch with them as to what is going on in your battles.

- Never forget the weapons of warfare that are at you disposal; prayer, praying in tongues, Scripture, praise and worship music, dancing before the lord, anointing with oil, and fasting.

- Monitor your body, mood, and attitude. These were the three areas I was able to detect an attack from the enemy, a shift in the spiritual atmosphere around me, or a move of God that was about to take place.

- Always do a cleansing prayer at the end of every battle you deal with. Plead the blood of Christ over yourself and remove any spiritual attachments from the enemy.

## Accepting God's Discipline:

All throughout my journey of I.D. and self discovery, God was disciplining me. In that discipline I had a choice; accept it or reject it. To accept it would cause me to press forward in my identity journey. To reject it would be to give up, thus leaving me stagnant in my personal/spiritual growth. His discipline comes in various ways, some we may be accustomed to, and some we may not. When you begin the process of sonship/daughtership I want you to be aware of the fact that there will be pain, discomfort, and hardships ahead of you. For any of you who have been disciplined you are well aware that it can be hard and even painful at times. It is a bittersweet thing that is needed but not necessarily desired. Yet this is the process we go through as we move from orphans, servants, or slaves to sons and daughters. If we look at Hebrews 12:5-11, we find that discipline is used by God for our benefit; "And have you completely forgotten this word of encouragement that addresses you as a father addresses his son? It says, "My son, do not make light of the Lord's discipline, and do not lose heart when he rebukes you, because the Lord disciplines the one he loves, and he chastens everyone He accepts as his son." Endure hardship as discipline; God is treating you as His children. For what children are not disciplined by their father? If you are not disciplined—and everyone undergoes discipline—then you are not legitimate, not true sons and daughters at all. Moreover, we have all had human fathers who disciplined us and we respected them for it. How much more should we submit to the Father of spirits and live! They disciplined us for a little while as they thought best; but God disciplines us for our good, in order that we may share in his holiness. No discipline seems pleasant at the time, but painful. Later on, however, it produces a harvest of righteousness and peace for those who have been trained by it."

As sons and daughters I want to encourage you to be open and accepting of God's discipline in whatever form it comes. For me it came in various forms and though it was difficult and painful at the time, I can honestly say that it was well worth it. I find it funny how in churches we always hear people desiring to know God more and to go deeper with Him into His heart and love. They cry out to know Him as the loving Father that He is and be conformed into the image of Christ. Yet as soon as the Spirit starts to work on people and they experience trials and hardships they begin to grumble and complain. They start to question God and ask Him why He is allowing all of these things to happen to them. Why is He putting them through these painful moments, why does it feel like He has abandoned them, why are we going through so much spiritual warfare? Yet at the same time we forget that we were the ones who went to God and asked Him to draw us closer to Him and make us like His son. We desired to be transformed but did not fully realize the refining process it required to get there. Many people will look up at Mt. Everest and desire to climb it all the way to the top, but do they recognize the stamina, endurance, perseverance needed to make it to the top? Do they know all that they will have to go through in order to accomplish something many have attempted but few have succeeded at? Count the cost my friends, as this process will stretch and pull you in ways you never thought possible.

For me this discipline included; 4 long years in the desert, being placed with different ministry teams at the last minute, suffering through food poisoning for a month, going through inner healing, internal spiritual warfare, countless sleepless nights, high levels of culture shock, humbling myself, repenting of the past, asking for forgiveness, as well as wrestling with God. Yet I count all of this worth it as it brought me to the place of knowing who I am in Him. At any time during this process I could have called it quits and threw in the towel. I could have given up, left the Middle East and India and told God I was done. But had I done this, I never would have entered sonship. I never would have known Him as the good, loving Father that He is. It is human nature, or rather the fleshly desire, to want to take the easy path rather than the difficult path. I had to continuously choose to say "no" to my flesh and continue on the hard path. I had to want God and be known as His son much more than the flesh's desire to stop pressing forward. It was a continuous uphill battle, but the more I fought it the easier it became. The more I saw the benefit of His discipline and the work He was doing internally, the easier it became to press forward with Him and not give up. While you are on your own journey, there will come times when you want to give up, when you feel the pressure, stress and warfare is too much to bare. But I want to encourage you to press on regardless of how much it hurts. No matter how difficult the climb up the mountain becomes, do not give up. Do not slow down, do not turn back. Others may surrender and call it quits who are also on the same journey as you; do not follow their lead but rather follow Christ's lead. Press on running the race, obeying the Father's voice and the Spirit's leading as it will bring you into His glory. Fear nothing as you die to your old self and step out into your true I.D. It is important to keep in mind at all times that God is doing this for your benefit, because He loves you, and desires for you to live as a son/daughter rather than an orphan. None of us want to be labeled as illegitimate children, especially when it comes from the King of Heaven. We all desire to be citizens of His, sons and daughters that hold an eternal royal lineage. But are we willing to pay the price in order to be labeled as such?

Accept and embrace the Father's discipline. Know that He is with you through it all, He is healing you, bringing out the best in you, and restoring your I.D. Know that the end result produces an abundant harvest above and beyond what we could ever imagine. The end result will be your sonship/daughtership.

## The Dark Night of the Soul:

There is one final aspect I want to discuss with you that for some of you will resonate deeply with your life. It is the theme of "The

Dark Night of the Soul," which is something I went through on occasion while traveling in the Middle East/India and contemplating my identity.

I have often heard people talk about the "dark night of the soul". It is a time when we are going through so much anguish or torment inwardly that our soul feels as if it is being ripped apart. It is during these times that our spiritual walk may become dry and at times even dead. But one thing I have learned and what others have taught me is that the length of the dark night is up to us. How long we choose to live out the dark night of the soul is our own personal decision. We can choose to go through it for weeks, months, or even years. This does not mean that during this time we are not saved or cannot function to some extent in life, but it does limit us within our Spirit. During the dark night of the soul we may not be hearing from God at all, and going to church or reading the Bible may have no effect on us. However, I have learned that for those who choose to live with an orphan heart, they will suffer longer through the dark night than that of sons/daughters. One of the reasons this is, is because sons/daughters know that they can go directly to their Father to deal with issues. They have direct access to the throne room and can enter in broken and destitute and allow their Father to revive them. Those who do not have a solid I.D. in Christ and who remain living under the orphan Spirit will often wander through life, going through the motions during their dark night. They will only be able to function at a basic level. Whereas those who live as sons and daughters will still be able to feel some time of closeness to God and connect with Him at some level. Even during this time, they will still feel joy, happiness, desire and drive for life that orphans do not feel. One thing that sons and daughters will recognize during this time is their need to do inner healing work so as to come out of their current spiritual stagnation and torment. There are many dangers in choosing to remain under the dark night of the soul. One of them is the power of hate. Hate is a powerful emotion that can enter in and take control of us if we allow it. It is even more so when the soul is in deep hurt, pain, torment, or anguish. When we are engulfed with spiritual warfare and demonic attacks in such ways we have never felt before, there is great potential for the enemy to enter in. Why does this happen? Because we allow our heart and soul to be filled with so much hate to drown out the pain that we are feeling, and it leads us to do unspeakable things.

I have found that the dark night of the soul is something that we all go through in this lifetime. I would even venture to say that Jesus went through His own dark night of the soul while in the Garden of Gethsemane. In Mathew 26:36-42 we find Jesus is in agony over what is about to come. His soul was deeply grieved to the point of death. He knew what had to be done in order for wrong to be made right and for salvation to come to all humanity. But to endure not just the crucifixion but the journey that let up to the cross, was more than any of us would want to bear. To have His soul grieved to the point where His flesh was sweating drops of blood has to be one of the darkest nights of humanity for any soul. Yet Jesus, secure in who He was as a Son and knowing who His Father in Heaven was, went forth saying, "not my will but yours be done." Jesus being the true son of God went through the dark night of the soul and overcame. And because He overcame we too can overcome through Him.

My brothers and sisters, we all have times where we go through the dark night of the soul. We have all been through these valleys for various reasons. But I can testify to this, that going through this time period is so much more easy as a son than as an orphan. When my I.D. is solidified in Christ, the dark night is still a rough time period, yet I know beyond a shadow of a doubt that the dawn is just around the corner. There is a light at the end of the tunnel. It is Christ who went before me and is calling me out to greater victories.

## Final words/Personal challenge:

If there is one thing I desire for you the reader it is this; that you push yourself so deep into the heart of God that you loose whoever you are and become who you were always meant to be! Conform your Identity to the Identity of Jesus Christ. Know who you truly are in the Father's love. It will not be easy, but it is worth it. I challenge you to start living life *with* God and run this amazing race called "life" *with* Him. Know Him so deeply and intimately that nothing in this universe can shake the ground you stand on. If you have ever seen the movie *The Hobbit*, there is a scene in the beginning where Gandalf is encouraging Bilbo to go out on an adventure, and Bilbo asks Gandalf, "Can you promise that I will come back?" And Gandalf replies, "No, and if you do you will not be the same." My friends, there is no promise that you will return from this journey of discovering your true identity. As you wrestle with finding your value, worth, approval and ultimately your true self, you will encounter physical, mental, emotional and spiritual challenges. There was never a promise for me as I traveled throughout the Middle East and India that I would ever come back. And though I did come back, I am not the same person I was when I left. But you must remember, that nothing worth having ever comes easy!

As you wrestle with your I.D and sonship/daughtership, I want to remind you that God disciplines those He loves. Please never forger this as it is vital to solidifying your I.D. in Christ. If He did not love us He would leave us as orphans wandering in this world without a home. But it is because that He loves us that He has no problem disciplining, correcting or even rebuking us so we stay on the right path. His discipline may be difficult to accept sometimes. As you learn and grow as His sons/daughters, He may ask you to let go of things that you desire because He knows they are not good for you. He may even take some things away from you because they would ultimately lead you away from Him. I want to encourage you during these times to accept His discipline as it is much needed. Although we think we know best, the truth is we don't, He does. I have found His discipline is not meant to harm me, but to refine me into the beloved son He desires me to be. Even though it can be hurtful and painful at the time, when we look back we can see how He was actually protecting us and keeping us from getting hurt. It is my hope that you will ask Him to discipline you so that you may be known as His. Though it is not an easy task, the Spirit of the Most High God will lead and guide you. He will bring you through the lowest valleys, the highest mountains, and into the place of restoration and peace with the Father. Spiritual freedom is a gift, but just like any other type of freedom, it has a price. Be willing to pay that price to truly know ones self.

Final warning: At the beginning of this book, I offered a warning to you that if you did not want your worldview, Identity and life challenged, that you should read no further. Now I offer you another warning; that if you choose not to push yourself, and push your I.D. deeper into Christ, then you will remain in the same state of affairs spiritually, mentally, and emotionally. If you are not willing to deal with things of the past, go through Inner Healing, open yourself up to God in every possible way, and participate in spiritual warfare, then you may never know your true I.D along with your full potential in Christ.

## Final Words:

If there is any encouragement I can give you it is to take the plunge and be willing and open to working on your Identity. Even if you feel that you have arrived at the place of truly knowing yourself in relation to God, probe a little bit and see what comes up. Never be afraid to improve oneself, to learn, grow and become more in Him than you already are.

## Helpful Resources:

Many of these resources helped me greatly in my own quest. Though I do not always agree with everything these authors say, they still have amazing insight.

> *A more Elite Soldier: Pursing a Life of Purpose*, Chuck Holton (This book helped me understand that my military experiences can empower me to press forward in difficult circumstances.

## AN IDENTITY REVEALED

*Experiencing a Fathers Embrace,* Jack Frost (This book helped me see God apart from legalism)

*Spiritual Slavery to Spiritual Sonship,* Jack Frost (This book helped me greatly in realizing that we all at times are living as spiritual slaves and the various ways in which we can move into sonship)

*From Orphans to Heirs: Celebrating Our Spiritual Adoption,* Mark Stibbe (This book helped me understand in greater depth what it means to be adopted by God)

*Who Switched Off My Brain? Revised: Controlling Toxic Thoughts and Emotions,* Dr. Caroline Leaf (This book helped me understand that holding onto the past or toxic thoughts/emotions are detrimental to oncs identity and growth)

*Escaping the Matrix: Setting Your Mind Free to Experience Real Life in Christ,* Gregg Boyd (This book helped me understand the mental traps we may be entangled in spiritually and not even realize it)

*Me the Me I Want to Be,* John Ortberg (This book helped me to see the future me, who I want to become, and how to get their)

*The Return of the Prodigal Son,* Henri Nouwen (This book helped me examine the different aspects of living as the prodigal son and how to step out of that mentality)

*In the Name of Identity: Violence and the Need to Belong,* Amin Maalouf

*The Father Heart of God,* Floyd McClung

*Healing the Orphan Spirit,* Leif Hetland

"Lost Without You—*The Story of Noor*" subtitled, "A Lebanese Girls Search for Identity," Kate McCallum. (This book helped me understand what refugees go through and their quest for belonging in relation to identity)

# Bibliography

Allers, Roger, and Rob Minkoff, dirs. *The Lion King*. Burbank, CA: Walt Disney Pictures, 1994.
Jackson, Peter, dir. *The Hobbit: An Unexpected Journey*. Burbank, CA: Warner Bros. Pictures, 2012.

www.ingramcontent.com/pod-product-compliance
Lightning Source LLC
LaVergne TN
LVHW051708080426
835511LV00017B/2786